TEACHING
OUR MEN
REACHING
OUR FATHERS

The Negro National Anthem

Lift every voice and sing
Till earth and heaven ring,
Ring with the harmonies of Liberty;
Let our rejoicing rise
High as the listening skies,
Let it resound loud as the rolling sea.
Sing a song full of the faith that the dark past has taught us,
Sing a song full of the hope that the present has brought us,
Facing the rising sun of our new day begun
Let us march on till victory is won.

So begins the Black National Anthem, by James Weldon Johnson in 1900. Lift Every Voice is the name of the joint imprint of The Institute for Black Family Development and Moody Press, a division of the Moody Bible Institute.

Our vision is to advance the cause of Christ through publishing African-American Christians who educate, edify, and disciple Christians in the church community through quality books written for African-Americans.

The Institute for Black Family Development is a national Christian organization. It offers degreed and nondegreed training nationally and internationally to established and emerging leaders from churches and Christian organizations. To learn more about The Institute for Black Family Development write us at:

The Institute for Black Family Development
15151 Faust Ave.
Detroit, Michigan 48223

AFRICAN AMERICAN CHURCHES

TEACHING
OUR MEN
REACHING
OUR FATHERS

MATTHEW PARKER

CONTENTS

ACKNOWLEDGMENTS

This book was a collaboration. I'd like to acknowledge those who worked directly on this project to bring it to fruition:

Dr. Lee June, Vice-President, Michigan State University, who helped design the surveys;

John Wallace, Assistant Professor, University of Michigan, who helped design the surveys;

Dr. Ken Canfield, President, National Center for Fathering, who was involved in survey design and data collection;

Dr. Leon Wilson, Professor, Wayne State University, who helped interpret and summarize survey results;

Joseph Williams, President of the Transition of Prisoners, Inc. organization, for sharing their case study;

Pastor Haman Cross Jr., of Rosedale Park Baptist, who shared the School of Ministry case study;

The 300 Summit Network leaders, who helped distribute and collect the surveys;

Diane Reeder of Written Images, who talked me through some of the chapters and edited the manuscript;

Finally, my wife Karon, and my five children, Matthew Jr., Tiffany, Michael, Kelly, and Justin, who teach me every day what it is to be a man and a father. I am grateful for their love and support in so many ways.

INTRODUCTION

T his book is the result of a collaboration that began many, many years ago. From my earliest years with my father, I have been blessed with African American role models who have shaped my view of life, as well as my character.

I must thank Barbara ("Mama") Walton, a mature and seasoned older woman, who provided direction without destroying my self-worth— often a fine line to walk when dealing with young African American men. My spiritual father, Dr. Lloyd Blue, helped me to understand the church's impact on the self-image of African American men. I have learned much from him.

The world will try to claim that these kinds of role models do not exist. You certainly do not see much of them in the communications vehicles that reach most of us today: newspapers, magazines, radio, and especially television! But they do exist, and sadly, that story has only faintly been told. We have tragically neglected the celebration of our heroes, both past and present, and it is time to reverse that. We have also neglected the African American male, who is nearly invisible until he commits a crime. It is time to reverse that, too.

We don't have to look too hard to see the enemy's strategy. To conquer a people, the first step is to control the male. Destroy his opportunity to become a man, deny him the information and support he needs to fulfill his responsibilities, and you can subdue an entire nation.

What I have attempted to do in this book is to focus attention on solutions and not just problems. You will see more than statistics here. You will see historical perspective. You will see original research from surveys that help us quantify the impact of the African American church on African American men, boys, and fathers. You will see some practical "how-to" information to introduce programs that address the particular issues and concerns that affect African American men and boys. You will see detailed case studies on some of the programs that already exist. It is my hope that you replicate these ideas in your own communities. "A little yeast rises the whole loaf" is a concept that can work to our benefit, if we can manage to spread useful information where it is most needed.

I hope this book becomes one of many vehicles to help our churches reach and teach African American males and cultivate among them leaders —leaders of families, of churches and ministries, and ultimately of nations. The Word of God says that the earth groans to see the sons of God revealed (Romans 8:19–22). The efforts you see described in this book are working to make that happen in the African American community.

I've learned a lot while working on this project. I see a pattern emerging as I have visited and talked with ministries nationwide. The bottom line is that any effective Christ-centered program must address some key issues if it is to bear fruit in the African American community with African American men and boys.

First, we must challenge them with this question: "What will you do with Jesus?" Our men must know that they have to be connected to the vine in order to be effective.

Secondly, we must teach heritage. Our men and boys must know their generational heritage as well as their African American heritage. They have to understand and be able to interpret the past in light of scriptural principles.

Third, there must be an academic and career component. We must challenge our boys at an early age with the question: "What do you want to do with your life?" And we must never stop asking that question. It is the critical question of our age.

Fourth, we must teach our males their responsibility as men—for their families, their communities, and their nation. Leadership means responsibility, and we must stress that a great-sounding title is meaningless unless you live up to it.

Finally, we must provide a connection between generations. I have found that the most effective programs are intergenerational. They allow the generations to come together—in service to each other and the larger community, in sharing, and in friendship. The generations have much to learn from each other; the "generation gap" does not have to be as hostile as we expect it to be.

It is my prayer that this book will be used effectively by those who wish to make a real impact on the African American male community by making disciples of boys, men, and fathers. I invite you to walk that journey with me, in all of your various capacities. It will produce the greatest blessing you could imagine!

CHAPTER 1

IN THE BEGINNING

In August of 1619, Antony and Isabella Pedro and 17 other Africans stepped ashore to what is now the state of Virginia and thus began the history of Africans in America. Antony and Isabella were married and in 1623 or 1624 gave birth to the first African American child: a boy named William, who was baptized by the Church of England.

They came, these first African Americans, as indentured servants and enjoyed the same status of White indentured servants who sold their services for a stipulated number of years. The available evidence suggests that most of this first generation of African Americans worked out their terms of servitude and were freed.

But the history of African American males reaches back much further, into the distant past when the great African Sudanese empires of Ghana, Akrum, Mali, Songhai, Meroe, Egypt, and Ethiopia flourished on the African continent. Lerone Bennett Jr., in his book *Before the Mayflower,* says:

"It is already reasonable, in fact, to believe that the African ancestors of African Americans were among the major benefactors of the human race.

Blacks, or people who would be considered Blacks today, were among the first people to use tools, paint pictures, plant seeds and worship gods. They founded empires and states. They made some of the critical discoveries and contributions that led to the modern world."

The African American male of today is considered an icon, a hero in the areas of sports, music, and dancing. Despite stellar achievements in these and many other areas, the image of the African American man is negative and no one seems immune to that characterization. African American men are automatically suspect. They are often judged without a trial or jury—even before all the facts come to light.

There is very little awareness of the contributions that African American males have made to science, medicine, history, and civilization. The National Task Force on African American Men and Boys, chaired by activist and former United Nations Ambassador Andrew Young, published "Repairing the Breach," which identifies a number of African American males who have succeeded at all levels of American society. The report points to Dr. Benjamin Carson, a world authority on brain surgery and the first neurosurgeon to successfully separate Siamese twins joined at the head. It mentions Colin Powell, the first African American ever to head the post of Chairman of the Joint Chiefs of Staff and now President George W. Bush's Secretary of State. It heralds Garrett Morgan's invention of the traffic light, making urban travel safe for all.

One common thread unites our many past and present Black heroes: They all had to overcome tremendous obstacles and take on singularly difficult challenges. Let us continue to remind America, African American people in particular, and the world that one of the great characteristics of the African American male is his ability to overcome all challenges—past, present, or future.

At one time, the African American church was a strong, pervasive, and revered institution. Boys who had no problem stealing, cheating, and purse snatching wouldn't dare pursue their illegal activities in the proximity of a church. While they might curse and fight in school, they would be careful to be polite to the preachers, the deacons, and the "mothers" in the church.

All that has changed drastically. There are reasons for this, and there are ways to address the problem. African American churches of today have a great opportunity for leadership in the spiritual, social, political, and economic development of African American males.

But first, we need to get a historical perspective.

The African American church movement started in the late 1770s with the founding of the first churches in South Carolina, Virginia, Philadelphia, Georgia, and New York. Churches were founded by free men and women as well as those who remained enslaved. The church was the place where leadership was taught and where people benefited from economic, political, and social education in addition to being taught the Word of God. God's Word was made relevant to the African American condition at the time. Most of our historical leaders came from the African American church. Throughout history, these churches provided social, political, economic, and spiritual leadership for many in the African American community.

It was a necessary development. After all, the Christian church established during the 200-plus years of African enslavement in this country was an overtly all-White, or all-European, institution with little or no room for persons of color. African Americans were not welcome. In fact, it may surprise some to learn that the legal prohibition against Blacks and Whites marrying was overturned only well into the Civil Rights Movement, in 1967 by the U.S. Supreme Court in the *Loving v Virginia* decision. At the time, 16 states still had that marriage prohibition on their books!

In fact, evangelical churches on the whole were diametrically opposed to any efforts to address the issue of racial equality from its first stirrings during the U.S.-sanctioned enslavement of Blacks to the Civil Rights Movement that began in the 1950s. It has been established that members of many White evangelical churches were actually also Ku Klux Klan members, and that pastors held the status quo of overt and covert racism even when the very concept became less and less popular as national policy.

The late Dr. Martin Luther King Jr. railed against what he called racism within the church. As reported in the landmark sweep of Civil Rights Movement history, *Parting the Waters,* author Taylor Branch quotes him as having ". . . wept over the laxity of the church." He was frustrated over racist incidents and those who held these attitudes, such as senior Episcopal Bishop C. C. Jones Carpenter. His great-grandfather a slave-holder in the 1840s and 1850s, Bishop Carpenter was a critic of segregation, but apparently unwilling to support the "Negro" protest movement. Taylor writes:

> "Carpenter needed to pick only the slightest difference with King in program or emphasis to stand aside (from the civil rights protests) . . . [he] chided King on the grounds that protest lacked Christian respectability, unaware of the countervailing storm within King of the Christian respectability of clergymen such as Carpenter himself." (*Parting the Waters,* 742)

Racism and inequality were rampant within churches of all denominations—most notably in the South, but in the North as well. And so, as Blacks began to question their status in American society and as churches, both Black and White, frequently failed to address these critical questions, men started to leave the church. Their reasons were varied. Some felt that people were more concerned about what they wore than the content of the message. Others saw hypocrisy in the leadership, where sins were kept secret and unaddressed. Others were embarrassed by their low or nonexisting incomes, especially when appeals were made for money.

Then there was the question of authority. Many men felt the preachers were too authoritative. A man who is made to feel inferior all week does not seek another setting where he is dominated.

African American males have a problem with submission; for many, it is an ugly word that reminds them of the oppression that they face every day. He feels that he gets no glory, no praise, no honor six days out of the week, and then he is faced with going to church on Sunday where all honor, glory, and praise belongs to God. Of course, God is worthy of praise, and He is to be extolled. However, there is a place for honoring people, and our men are on the bottom of that list.

Then, there is the problem of the missing male role model. The absence of an adult male is complicated by the mother's tendency to elevate her young son to a position inappropriate for his age and status in the home. By the time the male child is 12 years of age, the mother is many times already introducing him as "my little man" or the "little man of the house." In too many homes, a single mother is either too authoritative or not authoritative enough; thus the child grows up with an unhealthy attitude toward submission to women or anyone else, including God. The result is a male child who cannot or will not draw near to a God who requires submission for an authentic relationship. Noted author Jawanza Kunjufu, in his groundbreaking work, *Countering the Conspiracy to Destroy Black Boys,* describes this phenomenon in great detail. His now four-volume work should be required reading for all those who want to minister effectively to young Black men.

To make matters worse, sometimes wives and girlfriends would build up the preacher by talking about what a great man he was or repeating things that he said in his sermons. This created tension—a competitiveness, of sorts—and sometimes even a distrust of the preacher's motives. Too often, this kind of blind loyalty led women to be taken advantage of by certain unscrupulous preachers. Although held in such high esteem, these preachers did not always live up to the expectations of the congregation. The men in these women's lives would then get a very distorted view of Christians and ministers.

The messages that predominate do not help either. The man was often met with sermons pointing out male weaknesses and infidelity. He was too often belittled and met primarily with threats of hell's fire instead of with messages that imparted dignity, encouraged him, and built up his faith.

Many African American males won't even consider the salvation message, that Jesus is the only way to God, because today's church does not address their needs. The African American male needs money, job opportunities, business resources, and relevant skill training. The church collects money, but does little to create opportunities through which he can make more money. People often criticize men because of activities they engage in outside the church. If a lottery man, gambling man, or dope dealer tosses out an economic lifeline while the church stays on the shore, closed behind stained glass windows, repeating a sanctimonious agenda, it cannot expect to reach and save African American men. When our churches provide self-esteem, leadership development, economic relevance, and other positive initiatives, African American men will come.

As we enter the twenty-first century, a revival is underway in many of our African American churches. These churches believe that they can achieve something that no other institution or program has yet been able to do: recreate a place in African American families for men and, in so doing, give them the self-respect and moral confidence they need to become upstanding members of their communities. Getting African American men to church may be the single most important step to the preservation of African American people.

In this book, we will address some of these factors and look at ways that the African American Christian community—which includes churches as well as parachurch organizations—is stepping up to the responsibility of creating multiple generations of African American men who can impact our communities. But first, a chronicle of sorts. The next chapter, "The Journey," allows us to take a peek at how an African American boy becomes a man, and what happens at each stage of development.

CHAPTER 2

THE JOURNEY

Most children are born to loving parents. This is no less true in the African American community. Now we know that a loving environment is one of the best predictors of adult success—for men or women. So what goes wrong with our men? Why are African American men considered to be "at risk"? What happens along the way?

Obviously, there is no definitive answer. But there are clues. Clues that span decades. Clues that we observe every day in our communities.

In this chapter, we describe a common historical journey in the experience of a African American male child as he comes to manhood. This is not meant to be descriptive of every African American man who has ever lived; it is just a looking glass into an experience that serves to shape much of our population over the last 40–60 years. Obviously, much has changed since the '40s and '50s. But the lessons of history can be very instructive for us today.

Of course, some of the journey is positive. But things happen along the way. Let's look at this phenomenon—decade by decade—and see if we can find answers and perspective:

DECADE ONE—EARLY CHILDHOOD
Ages 1–10

A child is born to a loving mother and father, married or unmarried. The first five years go fairly smoothly. The young son is loved and nurtured. In fact, you may hear the mother or father talk about how smart he is. "Look, he can count to 10 already, and he's only 18 months!" Or, "See how attentive he is; only a week old, and already he's looking around!" The son is outgoing. He walks early, talks early. He is quite social and active, and loves to play and learn.

The parents and extended family respond with excitement. They interact with the child in accordance with their great expectations and impressions of his development. They believe the child is smart, and they give feedback that tells the child this as well.

Then, school begins. The young child enters kindergarten, and faces quite a different world. He enters a system that has not been designed to encourage his unique development. Suddenly, he faces a new and unknown community: teachers and school administrators that do not look like his parents, aunts, uncles, and cousins. At this point, some of the first impressions that he is "different" begin to develop. He doesn't know it yet, but every year from September to June he will embark on a slow process of assimilation—a process filled with potential pitfalls, but also with opportunities, if his caretakers and extended family are attuned to the risks inherent in the school system.

Here is the disconnect: the neighborhood is Black, but the institutions are White. This is true wherever the child goes—the school, the bank, often the corner store, and the restaurant. Power seems to be held by a community that is largely White.

Television reinforces this impression. Remember, the young child of the '50s and '60s has not watched very much television prior to starting school, as there was no Nickelodeon or Cartoon Network to provide 24-hour-a-day distractions. But by about five years of age, he discovers two exciting products: cartoons and commercials. The cartoons—think *Jetsons* and *Flintstones*—feature, once again, people who do not look like him or his family. While they may be entertaining, they still work to reinforce a worldview that unfortunately does not include him. The child does not even know this is happening, and often neither do his parents.

Back to school. Most of the staff are indeed White—most, that is, except the gym teacher and the janitor.* Virtually no African American teachers are found in the academic disciplines, such as math and science. In fact, even today, only two percent of the K–12 teachers are African American men, and the figure was much lower than that 20–30 years ago. What does that say to such an impressionable young man?

And don't forget history. Remember, this was largely before the movement to introduce African American studies to the schools. History was synonymous with Western Civilization; all other cultures were considered "Third World," "uncivilized," or "underdeveloped." Ironically, the individuals who peopled these lesser worlds looked more like our young student. His only heroes, token figures of American history, were Booker T. Washington and George Washington Carver.

Fortunately, though, this young child saw a very different picture in his own neighborhood. During that era, the era of the "baby boomer" child (born between 1946 and 1964), integration was only starting to even show up on the radar screen. That meant that different social classes of African Americans lived in the same community. The young African American child saw janitors and doctors conversing over the backyard fence. In some cases, he saw the benefits of a high school or even college education. While the school system and the media did not support what he was seeing at home, at least he saw it somewhere.

In this decade, the adage "It takes a village to raise a child" was not just a phrase people repeated. It was the reality. A strong moral and social value system permeated the neighborhood. Families believed in the same things, and those beliefs got reinforced everywhere the child went.

So, there is an initial "love affair" between parent and child; a community-wide reinforcing of key values and behaviors; and a burgeoning tension between the home/neighborhood reality and the reality of a larger society.

This was the case, right up to about the fourth grade.

*Remember: These are broad generalizations. All these realities do not hold true in every case; but they held true enough to influence an entire generation of African American men.

DECADE TWO—ADOLESCENCE
Ages 10–20

This school/community tension and divergence of the child's reality really starts to take hold when the African American male child reaches about the fourth grade. There is a reason for that. Developmentally, he is starting to explore his own decision-making process. He begins to question what he is told and taught. He begins to establish independence.

This is a normal and expected developmental phase. Many books on child psychology and teaching strategies attest to this. Good parents understand this and know how to deal with it. They are not caught off guard. If they have other children, they've seen it before. If they haven't, they have enough feedback from their extended family and the neighbors that they react appropriately to the situation—by encouraging questions while at the same time holding the line on rebellious behavior. But the questioning process, the desire to make independent decisions, is nurtured in an age-appropriate way.

It is not typically done this way by the school system, however. The largely White educators, to borrow one of today's slang phrases, "freak out" when they see a preadolescent African American male child start to establish independent behavior and thinking. Perhaps it's because their mindset does not have room for African Americans who question Whites for any reason. Perhaps the myth of African American male intimidation begins to take shape in their minds. Perhaps they've seen too many racist African "savage" movies. In any event, these sharp young men, who started out so bright and quick and active and happy, are now seen as a threat by their teachers at school and by the established order at large.

And they're still watching television—by this age, moving to the non-cartoon programming with even worse stereotypes of African Americans and Whites in terms of profession, intellect, and opportunity. At this time, other than the neighborhood, there are no other images to nourish the young African American male psyche.

Except in the church. Here, the leaders are largely African American men. They are respected, they are successful, they are available, and they teach. The church is the one place that American society of this time allowed African American men to exercise full leadership, authority, and responsibility. Here, the young African American male child sees African American adult men to look up to and admire.

It is at this point, the second decade, that we can take a page from Jewish history. After all, the Hebrew-African connection is strong. The African American and Jewish communities did not just start working together during the Civil Rights Movement. The connection goes back much, much farther than that. Here are a few brief historical observations to illustrate.

In the Book of Genesis, Noah had three sons: Ham, Japheth, and Shem. Ham was the father of Cush, Mizraim, Put, and Canaan. These four sons populated the continent of Africa; the sons of Ham gave birth to many of the non-Hebrew nations we see in Scripture, including the Hittites and the Moabites. Ultimately, these were the nations with whom the nation of Israel alternately fought and formed political and familial ties.

The Moabitess Ruth married Boaz and they had a son and named him Obed. He was the father of Jesse, who was the father of David; so she was also in the lineage of Jesus Christ. Ruth traces her roots to the continent of Africa through her ancestor Ham. Bathsheba, the woman with whom King David had an illicit affair, was a Hittite, a nation that also traced its roots to Ham. The Queen of the South, Sheba, head of a people and nation on the continent of Africa, visited David's son Solomon and took back some of his wisdom to her kingdom.

Going back even further than that, the first ancestor of the Hebrew nation, Abraham, fathered a child with the Egyptian (once again, on the continent of Africa) Hagar. The child produced by that union, Ishmael, went on to sire the Ishmaelite nations.

The prostitute Rahab, a Canaanite who protected the Hebrew spies as they sought to conquer the land of Canaan, eventually married a Hebrew and was another of Christ's ancestors.

When there was famine in the Promised Land, the patriarch Jacob took his sons and their families and sojourned to Egypt, where they were only to stay for a short time until the famine was ended. The generations after Jacob continued there until they grew so numerous that the Egyptian Pharaoh, intimidated, put them to work as enslaved people. But the Hebrews lived in Egypt for 400 years.

As we move to the New Testament, we see other evidences of

Hebrew-African ties. There is mention in the Book of Acts of the Ethiopian eunuch, whom the apostle Peter evangelized. He took the gospel to Ethiopia, then ruled in succession by a series of queens named Candace. It is said that this is the origin of the Coptic Christian Church.

We find other evidences as well. In the Jewish culture, there is the bar mitzvah, where a 12-year-old boy enters into manhood with many of its attendant responsibilities. To prepare, the boy must memorize the history of his people, attend a series of training sessions, and recite his knowledge at a special ceremony. Similarly, African culture has its own version, which is commonly known here as "rites of passage." Girls and boys who are 12 are put through special rituals and ceremonies to mark their coming of age and entry into adulthood. The Hebrew "clans" are analogous to the African "tribes."

So in both cultures, there is a clear line of demarcation between childhood and adulthood. Our Westernized culture has no such equivalent. And the price is paid by the African American male child.

Back to the fourth grade child. The African American male is moving toward an age where a "rite of passage" would be a valuable way to ensure his positive development. But what happens? The teachers see this questioning and curious young man on the verge of change instead as an "angry young man." They refuse to affirm his intellect and undermine his confidence at every opportunity.

The child born in the first half of the century, however, could still get plenty of affirmation in the neighborhood/community environment. After the 1960s, however, things began to change. The demographic shift from urban to suburban life created class divisions within the African American community from which we have yet to recover. In the urban core, role models began to disappear from the neighborhood. And that community "village" of parents, family, and church began to be supplanted by gangs.

Gangs in some neighborhoods are the only viable entities that affirm manhood for the adolescent African American male. They are the only entities that have a clear standard of conduct with discipline and a set of rewards and punishments to effect conforming behavior. Interestingly, it is the relationships that build the institution, and we learn from gang culture that the best way to build an institution is to focus on the relationships between people. We found that illustrated in the Underground Railroad. We often must explain to young children that the Underground Railroad that brought slaves to freedom was not actually a railroad, but instead a series of hiding places on a route to the northern United States and Canada. The escape route was built by people who cared about others and were willing to risk everything in the pursuit of justice. Again, they used what they had; they didn't need grants and edifices to carry out their important work. Like the Underground Railroad, gangs don't need bricks and mortar; their bricks and mortar are forged in group loyalty, community identity, and a shared purpose.

We see the devastating results of the gang culture today: substance abuse, crime, and lack of respect for authority—that is, adult authority; there is much respect for the authority of the gang leader!

In adolescence, the young man starts to consider ways to escape the 'hood, which is now a place of despair, apathy, and poverty. He considers sports and music first; he places most of his hope there, where the odds are nearly insurmountable. He also looks at crime: the opportunities more numerous, but the consequences riskier and less attractive. Religion becomes another viable option; he sees the affluent minister doing well and adds that to his list of options. Of course, there is the military. And then, often way down on the list, is education. After all, not many of his teachers have given him much of a chance of succeeding there. And again, we are not indicting the entire educational system, just making observations on some of the intractable and pervasive problems that exist.

DECADE THREE—COLLEGE AND BEYOND
Ages 18–30

The "baby boomer" generation found more of its ranks in college than any African American generation ever before. Once again, however, they found college to be a place of assimilation, not affirmation. The only exception to this rule was the Historically Black Colleges and Universities (HBCUs), where more teachers of color meant more affirmation, more role modeling, and more teaching of a multicultural history. An inclusive, family atmosphere, where students are nurtured and encouraged and paid attention to, was and is a typical HBCU experience.

At HBCUs, African Americans are encouraged to network with other African Americans. The experience is Afro-centric; African Americans are not punished for exhibiting race pride or for indicating a desire to address the societal issues that are part and parcel of institutionalized racism. In fact, such desires are celebrated and assisted by the educational institution. Contrast that to the majority institutions where such thinking is seen as "too militant" and frowned upon in an increasingly conservative campus climate.

Researcher Jacqueline Fleming is the author of *Blacks in College,* a groundbreaking study conducted in 1984 that compared Blacks in majority universities to Blacks in HBCUs. She said: "Convincing evidence has been marshaled to confirm that black students . . . show greater intellectual gains in predominantly black colleges."

Tragically, it is this period—the period from 12–30 years of age—where we see a precipitous decline in the number of males involved in the church. Churches who see this phenomenon and address it with rites of passage programs and initiatives targeted at young African American men can often dramatically affect this drop-off. They must be patient; it takes at least three years to completely alter a person's behavior.

DECADE FOUR—CAREER PHASE
Ages 30–40

On average, the African American male who earns a college degree does so between the ages of 21 and 28, so that by 30, they are ready to assume a significant place in the career market. Interestingly enough, in the Jewish culture, the age of 30 is significant in that 30 is the qualifying age to become a rabbi. Jesus' public ministry began at 30. After 30 years, you presumably have enough knowledge and training to be of useful service to society.

What has been going on during this time of preparation in the African American community? The father may be absent or uncommunicative about his role as protector and provider. He may not communicate to the son what it takes to succeed and how he overcame the obstacles placed in his path. This 30-year-old African American man, now armed with a degree that really signifies or suggests assimilation more than adequate preparation, ventures into the business world. He soon hits a wall.

The book, *The Black Manager,* by Floyd and Jacqueline Dickens describes the typical career phases for most African Americans:

1. Entry Phase—The person gets the job and believes it means that he is affirmed by those who hired him. Soon, the awareness of differences and distinctions based upon race become clear and bitterness can set in. The man in the newer, post-'60s generation, not having had a "village" experience, does not think to create a village at work with the older, seasoned African Americans who have weathered some of the same problems. In fact, these young career-minded individuals look down on the older African American worker. The "generation gap" phenomenon comes back to bite this lower-rung professional who fails to gain from others' knowledge.

2. Adjusting Phase—The person takes the attitude that he will do "whatever it takes" and actually starts to utilize the "village" concept. This helps, in some cases, to reduce the bitterness and give some hope that success is reachable.

3. Planned Growth Phase—The professional decides to seek out a mentor. The mentor is usually White; sometimes the mentor even "finds" him. This is most critical to ultimate career success. Mentoring's benefits include special assignments, access to top management, and exposure in the company. The person in this phase takes on conscious professional development. He wears the right clothes, joins the right clubs, buys the right home, even gets the "right" friends. At some point, however, he will have to decide how much of himself he is willing to sacrifice for success. He will have to consider whether success means trading in his African-American heritage to become completely assimilated.

4. Success Phase—At this point, the professional has a desire to help others. If he has made it this far, he feels somewhat magnanimous and looks around to see whom he can assist. The problem often is this: he has assimilated so completely into the corporate culture that he can no longer relate to those whom he most wishes to help.

DECADES FIVE AND SIX—MIDLIFE
Ages 40–60

At this point, the African American man, professional or not, college-educated or not, begins to sense his own mortality. He struggles with the question of legacy and his own importance to the world, or at least to the people around him. In addition, the professional struggles against the corporate "glass ceiling." He "knows" that he'll never "own the place," and for some that is supremely frustrating. Some, at this point, decide to try entrepreneurship. Others toil away in their positions, angry and isolated. They understand the conflict between keeping identity and pursuing success, and the conflict depresses them.

DECADE SEVEN—THE AGE OF WISDOM
Ages 65+

This can be the best age, if the above conflicts have been resolved satisfactorily—or it can be a time that is void and empty, if the earlier questions and frustrations have not been answered. At this age, the African American man should ideally be preparing to mentor the younger generation. If he has found a way to fulfill at least some of his dreams despite the ever-hovering specter of racism, he is free to pursue a role as mentor and "griot" (an African term that means "wise teacher"; it is this person who holds the repository of a tribe's history and culture).

OUR RESPONSE

We as African American men need to be asking ourselves, "What is the greatest thing I can do?" The answer should be clear and fire our passion and purpose: We need to make sure that our children and grandchildren and protégés form, like the faithful few who remained true to the one God of Israel, a remnant of those who have gained godly wisdom and won favor because of it.

God instructs us about this very thing in the psalms: "Make sure that the parents tell the children of My laws and ordinances, and that the children tell their children, so that there will be blessing in the land" (based on Psalm 78:5–6).

CHAPTER 3

SURVEYING THE LAND— THE BIG PICTURE

T he year 2000 was a year for surveys. The Institute for Black Family Development, jointly with the National Center for Fathering, conducted a national survey of African American men to discover their perceptions of themselves as fathers and of the status of African American fathers in general. Approximately 248 men from 10 states, more than 15 cities, and the District of Columbia responded to the survey. (Please review Table 3-1 for key demographic information on the survey respondents.)

In addition, the Institute for Black Family Development convened a select group of men and churches to gain perspective on their view of the church relative to its effectiveness in preparing African American boys, men, and fathers. These individuals and institutions were past participants in a biannual National Summit on Black Church Development, an event that allows for sharing of ideas and "best practices" within the African American church community. Past participants now form a "roundtable" to share resources and collaborate on efforts to evangelize and disciple our communities.

This chapter discusses the results of both surveys and gives some implications for action by the African American church.

JOINT SURVEY—INSTITUTE FOR BLACK FAMILY DEVELOPMENT/NATIONAL CENTER ON FATHERING

The joint survey focused on a demographic group that has often been ignored by social scientists as well as the media: African American men who are well educated, spiritual, and have been married to the same woman for a number of years. The table on the next page lists the findings.

As you can see from Table 3-1, this is a group of men who are well educated, Christian, with strong family histories and current family structures intact. According to their responses, these men maintained a high level of spiritual involvement and a good relationship with God as well as their children.

PERCEIVED STATUS OF FATHERING

Fathering in the African American community has been under scrutiny, if not direct attack, for sometime now. The media and, to some extent, popular literature present a picture of widespread deficiency. Too often the portrayals are not well supported by the data, but seen as factual because of the power of television, radio, newspapers, and magazines.

We set out to test a hypothesis: that there are a number of positive things going on relative to fathering in the African American community that are often unnoticed or not discussed. We did not set out, however, to unbalance the picture in the positive direction; we also asked about some of the problematic aspects of fathering.

We asked respondents to agree or disagree with the following statements:

- The most significant family or social problem facing America is the physical absence of the father from the home.
- Fathers today spend less time with their children than their fathers did with them.
- Most people have unresolved problems with their fathers.
- Most fathers know what is going on in their children's lives.
- Most fathers are doing a good job providing for their family financially.

TABLE 3-1. JOINT SURVEY DEMOGRAPHICS

Locations	Percent of Men Surveyed
Philadelphia, PA	18%
Washington, D.C.	17%
Detroit, MI	15%
Atlanta, GA	10%

Education	
Bachelors Degree	28%
Masters Degree	14%
Doctorate	3%

Education	
Experienced more than 6 months of unemployment	36%
Frustrated with job	40%
Not frustrated with job	57%
Considering a career change	40%

Average Age	40 years old

Marital Status	
Married	76%
Parents did not divorce	70%
Parents had a good marriage	40%
Parents had an average marriage	26%
Parents' marriage was poor	33%

Spiritual/Fathering Status	
Active Christians	89%
Hold a church office	60%
Share faith regularly	75%
Reconciled to God	89%
Reconciled with children	90%

- Most fathers are doing a good job providing a safe environment for their children to grow up in.
- Most fathers feel comfortable discussing spiritual matters with their children.

Table 3-2 shows the responses.

TABLE 3-2. SURVEY ON
THE PERCEIVED STATUS OF FATHERING

Questions	Strongly Agree	Agree	Disagree	Strongly Disagree
The most significant family or social problem facing America is physical absence of the father from the home.	55.7	33.6	9.0	1.6
Most people have unresolved problems with their fathers.	22.6	52.3	20.6	4.5
Fathers today spend less time with their children than their fathers did with them.	19.8	47.5	29.3	3.3
Most fathers know what is going on in their children's lives.	5.0	28.5	58.7	7.9
Most fathers are doing a good job providing for their family financially.	3.8	49.4	41.4	5.4
Most fathers are doing a good job providing a safe environment for their children to grow up in.	4.6	45.6	41.5	8.3
Most fathers feel comfortable discussing spiritual matters with their children.	7.0	22.2	53.5	17.3

A majority (89.3%) of respondents to the survey perceived the father's absence from the home as the most significant problem facing America. Almost three quarters (74.9%) of them thought that most people had unresolved problems with their fathers. Slightly more than two thirds (67.3%) agreed that today's fathers spend less time with their children than their fathers did with them. Only 33.5% of the fathers agreed that most fathers know what is going on with their children; but a slight majority (53.2%) of them thought that most fathers are doing a good job providing for their families financially. Respondents were almost evenly split in their response to whether fathers were providing a safe environment for their children. Less than 30% of the fathers agreed that "most fathers feel comfortable discussing spiritual matters with their children."

While there is a glimmer of hope, it is clear by the data that this survey is consistent with statistical realities in the African American community, where the majority of our children live in households headed by females.

Corresponding to the perception of father's absence is the significant number reporting that fathers in general spend insufficient amounts of time with their children. This is possibly a separate issue from that of a father's absence. Investment of time is a critical element of paternity. Given the complexity of our society, work demands, and related factors, it is even more important that fathers find creative ways to spend more time with their children. Since most of these respondents are fathers, this can be seen as a cry for help to find such ways. Remember, the fathers surveyed are primarily from intact homes. Their response is a clarion call to the church; we must teach fathers how to invest time with their children.

The issue of unresolved problems with fathers also raises another call to the church for an appropriate response. While the survey did not isolate the specific nature of the "unresolved problems," we cannot trifle away the reality that some intervention in this area may be needed. Resolving interpersonal difficulties within families is a skill that is teachable through venues such as workshops or seminars. Positive father/son relationships are critical to the successful integration of males into the society and for the perpetuation of healthy fathering.

Perhaps the most important response in this survey is the reported sense that most fathers are uncomfortable talking to their children about spiritual matters. This response may imply that fathers are not very involved in spiritual matters themselves. But it may also be an indication that the church needs to begin teaching fathers how to communicate such matters to their children.

This is not the easiest of tasks. To some extent the approach to such matters has always been corrective; after a wrong has been done, the preacher's involvement is solicited or the father begins a reprimand speech. But to teach spiritual values and biblical truths in a consistent and systematic way is much more difficult. A concerted effort is clearly needed to successfully engage fathers in a consistent, systematic way that teaches the process of teaching and imparting spirituality to children.

PERSONAL STATUS OF FATHERS

Another section of the survey attempted to get a sense of the respondents' own relationship with their fathers. Given the perception that unresolved problems with fathers is a major issue, understanding the relationship of the men in the survey to their own fathers was an important aspect of the study.

According to the results of the survey, 85% of the men said that they could list ways that they are different from their fathers. These results could be interpreted in two ways. First, the men could be dissatisfied with their fathers. Indeed, about half of the men reported that their fathers were not there for them during their formative years, and a similar number said that their fathers did not regularly share affection with them. These findings are interesting given the responses to another question about whether the survey participants wished for a different kind of father. When asked to agree or disagree with the statement, "I wish I had a different father," most of the men (72%) disagreed. Also, the majority of the men reported that they would like to be like their fathers.

Clearly, this survey presents a mixed picture. Less than a quarter of the men reported having some anger about the way their fathers treated them; about two-thirds of them thought their dads did the best job they could in raising them. These responses represent an interesting divergence which would be useful to investigate further. Why do the men aspire to be like the very fathers with whom they are dissatisfied? Why, in light of the overwhelming complaint of not enough time given by their own fathers, are they reluctant to indicate anger or dissatisfaction in general?

Next, let us take a look at the respondents' perceptions of their own fathering. Fifty-five percent of the men find fathering to be overwhelming, even though 92% reported that they tell their children that they love them. Many of them also said that they spend time with their children: 70% find time to play with them; 91% are involved in discipline; 92% pay attention when their children speak to them; 85% reported an even temperament; and 77% said they were consistent when dealing with their children.

Other fathering attitudes were reported positively as well. Most of the respondents (76%) thought they had no difficulty executing the fathering role and were highly motivated to do so. An overwhelming number of respondents (88%) claimed that they understand what expectations of their children are appropriate based on their level of maturity. However, a significant number (40%) of respondents said that they tend to delay doing the things they know they should be doing as fathers.

In terms of spousal relationship, approximately 80% supported the view that their marriages were "not in serious trouble." The same number reported that they are capable of calmly discussing differences that may exist in their spousal relationships. Moreover, 91% of the men reported that they tell their wives that they love them. It is within this framework that a little more than three quarters of the men disagreed with the proposition that their families were "being torn apart by outside influences." Additionally, 88% of the respondents said they believe that their wives "really love" them.

Does this data indicate that all is well in familial relationships? Certainly the picture presented here is not as devastating as is usually thought. Nonetheless, given that the population represented in this survey is largely Christian, with higher-than-average educational attainments, it is especially important that we look not only at the personal responses relative to their own situations but also at the perceptions they hold of fathering in the African American community at large.

We do not mean to suggest here that church attendance and reported spirituality is the ultimate panacea for family problems. Indeed as the data suggests, there are variations even among those who consider themselves spiritual. Nevertheless, there can be little dispute that commitment to church increases the possibility of success in other areas of life. The levels of involvement with children and family by the men in this sample do not accord with the patterns observed in the general population. This contrast strongly suggests that a spirituality does indeed positively impact family relationships and positive fathering.

"ROUNDTABLE" SURVEY

In the "roundtable" survey, we posed a critical question to African American men and to their churches who represent the "roundtable" in twelve cities across our nation: "What has the African American church done to prepare young men for manhood and fatherhood?"

For the individuals surveyed, we posed the question this way: "What has the church done to prepare you for manhood and fatherhood?" We found that the primary value that the church provided, from the individuals' perspectives, was the value of role modeling. Many of the respondents said that they joined the church late in life.

One man noted:
"In 20 years, I had never seen an African American man treat his wife like a queen."

And another:
"Boys learn better by observing—actions speak louder than words."

Others pointed to the centrality of the praise and worship service. One individual noted that the praise portion of the service was "just as important as the preaching—it actually affects my walk . . . if I'm worshiping God, I know I need to be living right."

Others spoke to having the chance to serve in leadership roles—opportunities to speak, manage, and organize were in abundance.

Cultural relevance and community involvement were also noted as a positive. The African American church, in addition to its focus on Scripture and doctrine, also provided significant information on African American history and culture that was not as easily obtained elsewhere. Others talked about the presence of the church as a servant, meeting various needs in the community.

However, many survey respondents indicated that they were not getting specific, focused, practical preparation for becoming a husband and a father. They spoke of not really knowing exactly what to do when faced with those roles. They also criticized what they called "hypocritical mentors," and suggested that male mentors who did not "walk the talk" served to stunt their spiritual growth. Many of the men indicated that their relationships with other Christian men lacked depth. Even though the church did provide a safe and supportive environment for hurting souls, men did not feel that they were receiving the information they needed to be more effective in their multiple roles.

As a result, they made recommendations. Here are a few:

- Men married 10 years or longer should teach the "younger" married men.
- Movie nights would help to "break the ice" and facilitate meaningful relationships.
- The church should seek to identify the "real" needs of African American men.
- Skill development should be a focus: career fairs and information on how to be professionally successful.
- The church should focus on more "team building" between men, fostering friendships, and discipleship.

Other suggestions included retreats and activities with other ethnic communities. "The church needs to fight cynicism and demonstrate relevance," said one respondent. Said another: "This is a journey, not a race." Only one respondent indicated that an African American church made no difference in terms of their spirituality or development. "My faith would be no less intensive in another environment," he indicated.

The survey of the churches yielded some responses that echoed the individuals' but with a decidedly different perspective. All of the churches surveyed indicated that they had some level of premarital counseling, ranging from four sessions up to 5–6 months of ongoing counseling for engaged couples. The initiatives seem to be working; one church reported fewer than five divorces in 20 years since premarital training was instituted.

Some of the churches responded that they did not have significant programming in place for single people. With our current downward trend in marriage and upward trends in divorce, the church is populated with more and more people who are not married or have never been married; so the focus on singles must become more important if the church is to remain relevant to the human condition.

Many of the churches pointed to significant family initiatives, however. They reported implementing cell and discipleship groups, designating a "Family Emphasis" month, regular social activities, annual "husband/father" seminars, and including information on fatherhood in their deacon's training. One pastor indicated that he and his wife worked specifically to model a healthy marriage in their congregation.

In terms of youth programming, the churches pointed to extensive use of video, especially for men and young people, who tend to be less likely to read; and the use of drama as a teaching tool. One church reported that it had instituted what it called the "Cornelius Award" for strong male leaders in the church.

In terms of their church's composition, the responding churches reported that the composition was beginning to mirror societal problems. Many churches reported that couples living together without benefit of marriage was a significant problem. One church indicated that it instituted church discipline if the couple did not change their living arrangements or marital status after a reasonable period of time.

Additionally, churches reported that blended or single-parent families often outnumbered traditional families. They indicated that they were moving toward instruction that addressed this growing phenomenon.

TABLE 3-3. INDIVIDUAL SURVEY QUESTIONS

- How has the African American church helped you in developing as a man?
- How has the African American church helped you in preparing for adulthood?
- How has the African American church helped you in your faith?

- How has the African American church helped you in preparing to be a husband?
- How has the African American church helped you in preparing to be a father?
- What would be your recommendations to the African American church to improve their programs targeted at African American males?

TABLE 3-4. CHURCH SURVEY QUESTIONS

- What is your church doing to develop the faith of its men? List any programs or events that are touching men's lives (i.e., Bible studies, leadership training, evangelistic outreach, rites of passage programs, mentoring, or specific classes). Please include approximately what proportion of your total church is male and how many men participate in the program.
- What is your church doing to promote family enrichment? Describe the different types of family situations that are common in your church (like traditional, blended families, single-parent households, live-in arrangements, etc.). Are there classes or aids offered to strengthen these households? How effective are these programs?
- How is your church training and equipping fathers? List specific ways fathers are being equipped to meet the needs of their children. Include ideas or strategies fathers are using to reach out to the "fatherless" in the congregation.
- What is being done to promote marriage and positive male/female relations within your church? Describe the premarital helps you utilize to guide young people into a marriage. What is being done to reach out to singles who have no spouse?
- What tools would be most useful in helping your church strengthen its families? List the all-time best three events, conferences, or classes that were life changing in your church life experience. Additionally, how should these tools be delivered (e.g., videos, books, classes, visiting speakers, etc.)?
- Please review your responses to the previous five questions and tell us what we've missed with respect to strengthening the families in your church.

REACHING OUT

We've talked a lot about teaching our African American men, boys, and fathers. Let's now look at strategies for reaching them.

The curricula mentioned in the later chapters of this book are specifically designed to address male needs. In his book, *Reclaiming the Village: The African American Christian Man,* author Eddie B. Lane talks about man's four basic needs: family, a life mission, a social context that affirms his significance, and a relationship with God through Jesus Christ. The curricula we have highlighted in these chapters address all four of those needs.

Admittedly, we must first make sure that they come and that they are sufficiently attracted to our churches, organizations, and programs to make the effort to participate.

For older men, it's late in the game and their habits are set. The best way to reach African American male adults is by one-on-one interaction. Men will not always respond to even the most fervent appeals from the pulpit. Men who are connected to Jesus Christ and to a local church family must make the effort to evangelize other men on their jobs and in their neighborhoods. The best way for them to do that is through "relationship evangelism." As men, we have to make the effort to form friendships and relationships that go past the superficial level and put us in a position to be open with other men about our challenges and struggles, and to show and demonstrate how we have overcome them through our spiritual relationship and by following the wisdom outlined in the Word of God.

For our African American boys, it's a little different. At a young and impressionable age, they will automatically be more open to spiritual things. After all, Jesus did say that children seem to know best how to receive the kingdom of God. But still, we need a strategy here as well. Right now, the odds are not good for our boys. Once again, I cite Jawanza Kunjufu in his *Countering the Conspiracy to Destroy Black Boys, Volume III.* He indicates that, while gangs, drug dealers, and the media command 2–8 hours of our young men's time per day (a figure that increases, rather than decreases, with age), parents, community groups, and church attendance together average a paltry 7–34 minutes per day—a figure that *decreases* with age. It is no wonder our young men are in trouble!

We will need a concerted effort to reverse this trend. Of course, it goes without saying that fathers must make their presence known in the home. But what about the African American women who are heading households without a man present in the home? According to Lawson and Thompson, approximately 44% of African American households are headed by females—either through out-of-wedlock births, death, or divorce. The 2000 U.S. Census Data indicates that 62% of African American children live in single-parent households, more than 90% of them headed by females. Nearly 40% of those households are at or below the poverty level.

This is where the church can build upon the unique strengths of the African American family. Lawson and Thompson suggest that the African American culture is uniquely known for its tendency to form close extended family ties. Grandparents, aunts, and cousins often live with mother, father, and children, or at least interact frequently. The church must find ways to continue this trend and extend it where it no longer exists in certain families. If the grandparents are deceased or, as is frequently the case, live in another geographical area, the church should provide a venue for older members to serve as surrogate grandparents. This could be done through the venue of church meals or major events or through adopt-a-grandchild programs.

In addition, we must have African American men involved with boys at an early age. Think outside the box. What if churches developed Sunday school programs that were more gender-specific, with young African American boys, as early as 3 years of age, being taught by African American men? What a powerful statement that would make, and what an opportunity to impact and influence a young mind!

As you can see, surveys are helpful in identifying needs and assessing outreach efforts. Keep these strategies in mind as you read the next few chapters. In these chapters, you will find some concrete, usable teaching and planning tools.

CHAPTER 4

STARTING A MALE AND FATHERING PROGRAM

INTRODUCTION

If you give a man a fish, he will eat for a day. If you teach a man to fish, he will eat it for a lifetime."

The most effective way to successfully implement a program in the African American community is to gain the respect and trust of the targeted community and provide its residents the potential for empowerment. The African American community wants to eat for a lifetime, so it is imperative that they learn to fish. African American churches can provide that opportunity. These churches sustain the heavy burden of service to the community. Fully owned by African Americans, they are often the sole institutions in communities of color that represent and provide stability. They are, many times, primary sources of day care and after-school activities, tutoring programs, safe havens from distress, community development and empowerment activities. African American churches customarily represent the community in the arenas of public policy, housing, and citizen participation in the nation's civic life.

For maximum effectiveness, it is imperative that male and fathering programs come from African American churches, the foundations of strength in the African American community. This institution has a reputation for noteworthy achievements and credibility, as well as access to the African American community. When this happens with a critical mass of initiatives, the result will be the most substantial national network of institutions within the African American community.

Religious charity has always been a predominant part of the volunteer community. Today, the high correlation between religion and voluntarism is fundamental and attributable to the stability, credibility, and availability of leadership in the church. Male and fathering programs that seek maximum effectiveness would do well to collaborate with this established, historical, and venerable institution. Here, we propose a way to begin.

STEP ONE: KNOW YOUR COMMUNITY

Male and fathering programs that want to make an impact on the African American community must first embrace that community. An effective outreach program that incorporates evangelism and discipleship through the church is the place to start.

The effort should begin with a comprehensive needs assessment of the target community. African American churches should never assume knowledge of a community's needs without first asking the members of that community.

Programs should be ultimately geared toward the development of a manual so that the effort can be replicated elsewhere, as well as repeated in the sponsoring church. We tend to focus on the program and fail to see our efforts as a tool for impact in a wider geographical area than just our own neighborhoods. The program oversight committee should identify an editor specifically to organize this effort and employ other professionals in various areas as needed to contribute to the manual.

STEP TWO: WRITING A PROGRAM PROPOSAL

A proposal is a tool, an integral step in the planning and developing a successful program. It helps generate financial and other resource investments for your ministry and is crucial in the introduction and communication of your program to staff, volunteers, members, leaders, donors, and other interested program parties.

Think of the proposal as a contract to deliver goods or services that a community or population needs and your organization is responsible to render. Make it clear, concise, powerful, and dynamic. Here is a way to proceed:

Develop a Vision Statement—This represents the embodiment of your entire program. Your long-range goal should be to become recognized as the leading source of assistance and information on African American men and fathers over a given time period and in a given geographic area. Your vision statement will assist in providing a common focal point for your staff and your target population, charting a future course and answering these questions: Who? What? Where? Why? When?

For churches, the Vision Statement should have a clearly defined biblical basis. It would be helpful to adopt a key Scripture to go along with your statement that relates to the vision.

Develop the Narrative Section—All proposals differ slightly, but include the following basic elements:

Need Statement—An explanation and rationale for your male or fathering program that describes the need to be addressed. This will include a definition of the target population that covers service area, as well as demographic information. The need statement is an important component because it demonstrates that the need is pressing and that improvements cannot wait. The emphasis is best shown by the use of:

➢ Statistics, particularly those applying to boys, men, and fathers in your area.
➢ Quotes from qualified and reputable leaders in the field.
➢ Personal accounts.

At the end of this section, you should introduce and explain the history, mission, and substantial accomplishments of your agency. If the church is relatively new, you might include the accomplishments of key professionals and/or management. You must be able to demonstrate that your church is worthy of funding and your work will be beneficial to boys, men, and fathers on a long-term basis.

Program Goals and Objectives—A description of your vision for the target population, as well as specific subgoals. What do you want to happen as a result of this program? What kind of change do you envision in the men and fathers that your program will impact? This section answers those questions. You also have an opportunity here to creatively explain the uniqueness of your methods and program design.

Implementation Timeline—A broad description of tasks to achieve program goals over a given time period (typically one year). This "method" section answers the following questions:

Recruitment Strategies—Answers the question, "How will you let people know about the services you provide and secure their participation?" This section details outreach and marketing strategies (e.g., promotional materials, press releases, newsletters, community information boards, or the Internet).

Organization and Staffing—Answers the question, "How is your program structured and staffed?" You should have a clear organizational chart and descriptions of all staff positions, including volunteers. Here, you would also describe the nature of any collaborative relationships, both formal and informal, with other churches and organizations.

Training—Addresses the question, "How competent is your staff?" This section describes how staff and volunteers will be trained.

Evaluation—This section answers the question, "How will you know whether the program was successful?" Once the scope of the program has been firmly established, the program assessment process and criteria must be developed. The strengths (assets) and weaknesses (needs) of the program must be reviewed. A thorough assessment covers both internal (within the program) and external (societal or other environmental influences) factors that impact the program. Useful points to cover include:

➢ What were the desired outcomes, benefits, and overall mandate of the program?
➢ Was the goal of the program accomplished through the service delivery outcome?

➢ Did your program remain within the confines of the established budget?

➢ Was the intended message effectively communicated to the target audience?

➢ Were complete and concise program records and documentation kept concerning the finances, program performance, community contact, and volunteer tracking?

➢ Did your program outcome meet your anticipated goals in terms of the number of people served?

In order to obtain an unbiased measure of the effectiveness of the program, a consultant could be selected to oversee the research, design, and implementation of the evaluation component of the program. Critical issues to be highlighted include the level of participation in the program; changes in knowledge, behavior, and attitude of the program participants; and ability of users to understand and make practical use of the manual.

Financial Section—This section details startup, equipment, staff, and materials costs; projects a budget for the given time period (usually one year); and details a fundraising plan. Some fundraising strategies include:

➢ Service fees
➢ Endowment program
➢ Membership fees
➢ Foundations
➢ Direct-mail campaigns
➢ Campaigns aimed at wealthy individuals

Conclusion and Appendices—Make a strong ending case for your male or fathering program that summarizes benefits. The appendices may include items such as:

➢ Research tables or graphs
➢ Key staff profiles
➢ List of board members

➤ Creditability builders: auditor's report, annual report, publications
➤ Recommendation and/or endorsement letters

STEP THREE: WORKING WITH THE PASTOR

Any individual or group of individuals within the church that seeks to start a program of this kind must understand the culture of their church and secure the participation and blessing of the pastor. An effective way to begin is to get on the pastor's agenda in order to explain the program. Once you receive the "green light" to start, you will have a clear path to excellent communications, program visibility, and effectiveness. We advise that you form a working group that includes professionals with expertise in the area to lend credibility to the program.

STEP FOUR: SELECTING A COORDINATOR

The coordinator is critical to the success of your male or fathering program. This appointed leader generates program interest, trains team members, and mobilizes congregational support and participation. It is protocol for the pastor to either appoint this person or designate the method of selection. The program should provide a job description of this position, as well as qualifications and desired personal characteristics to the appropriate church leadership.

Ordinarily, a coordinator is an involved member of the congregation, is known by the pastor, and is recognized and respected by the congregation. The coordinator ought to possess the following skills and attributes:

➤ *Leadership skills*—an effective coordinator has vision, is able to provide effective direction and guidance, can delegate responsibility, and is able to encourage and inspire others.
➤ *Organizational skills*—an effective coordinator has the ability to provide structure, make plans, and arrange meetings and activities.
➤ *Communications skills*—an effective coordinator can speak effectively, fluently, and comfortably with the pastor and congrega-

tion in the effort to provide and facilitate the exchange of information.

➤ *Experience*—an effective coordinator has directed and managed other programs within the congregation.

The specific roles of the coordinator include, but are not limited to:

➤ *Initiating enthusiasm and participation*—the coordinator must build the curiosity of the congregation in order to promote positive changes and create an atmosphere that encourages the involvement of the members.

➤ *Promoting the program to the congregation*—the coordinator gives visibility to the program via public announcements, as well as developing promotional messages, flyers, and bulletins.

➤ *Assisting with the training of team members*—the coordinator will work to give the team an overview and rationale for programs and provide or arrange for appropriate training.

➤ *Creating a program plan and timetable*—the coordinator will work with the team to develop the activities for the program, assign responsibilities, and maintain schedules in accordance with the timeline set in the preliminary stages.

➤ *Help carry out program evaluation*—the coordinator has the ability to ensure that a member of the team assists with distributing and collecting evaluation forms after every activity.

➤ *Working with businesses and organizations in the community* to solicit resources such as volunteers, educational brochures, and other materials.

STEP FIVE: TRAINING THE COORDINATOR

The preliminary step in training the coordinator is the personal, one-to-one orientation meeting between the coordinator and the pastor, covering the following topics:

➤ Goals of the male or fathering program.

➢ Relevant data, demographics, and risk factors relative to African American men, boys, and fathers—particularly in the area where the church is located.

➢ Description of the program and activities involved.

➢ Successful male and fathering programs in other churches that have similar goals.

➢ Roles, responsibilities, and experiences of every player in the program.

➢ Communications plan with the pastor and congregation to keep those involved informed, alert, and interested.

➢ Any other information pertinent to the successful implementation of the program.

STEP SIX: SELECTING THE TEAM

The pastor usually appoints the team members or announces the formation of a team followed by recruiting volunteers from the congregation. Teams selected and appointed by the pastor are usually able to secure increased support and operate at higher levels of performance. It has also been shown that members who are well known and trusted by the pastor and congregation usually achieve the highest success in implementing programs and securing the participation of their fellow church members.

The program team ought to be comprised of individuals with excellent interactive skills, who are willing and able to be trained and have a genuine interest in related issues. These persons must also be willing to make time commitments for training and assisting with program activities. The success of the team relies in large part on clearly defined expectations and the sense that their efforts are needed and appreciated.

A diverse group of people possessing an array of skills and backgrounds can contribute to the program and assist the team tremendously. Members of the congregation who are also trained in various aspects of program management can provide valuable technical assistance in a wide variety of program areas.

STEP SEVEN: ORIENTING AND TRAINING THE TEAM

Team members must be involved in and have ownership of all aspects of the program, including planning, recruiting volunteers, preparing promotional materials, meeting with community groups for assistance, setting up activities for implementation, and evaluating the effectiveness of the program. For this to happen, they must also fully understand the program. The role of the program coordinator in this instance is to convene a group orientation covering the following topics:

➤ Roles, responsibilities and expectations
➤ Goals of the program
➤ Confidentiality issues
➤ Assessment of team members' skills and talents
➤ Experiences in other congregations
➤ Other background information

Following the orientation, subsequent training sessions should emphasize educating the program team about effective ways for the team, coordinator, congregation, and pastor to work together in order to achieve program goals. The team must devise strategies for planning, managing, and implementing the program. Team members should be assigned specific tasks tailored to their distinct skills and talents, and a timeline should be developed.

In an effort to maintain appropriate points of contact, lines of communication need to be delineated upon the delegation of responsibilities. Regular meetings should be identified and finalized upon completion of the training.

STEP EIGHT: SURVEYING THE CONGREGATION

In order to adequately provide the team with baseline information on the demographic characteristics, knowledge, interest, and availability of church members, a survey of the congregation is necessary. This information will give the team the opportunity to identify and target risk factors and select activities that will appeal to the greatest population and attract maximum participation. This survey will also provide helpful data for scheduling program events at the most convenient times for team members and the congregation.

The survey ought to include the following components:

➢ Age
➢ Gender
➢ Understanding and identification of modifiable risk factors
➢ Interest in education and intervention activities
➢ Availability for participation in education and intervention activities

The method by which a survey is administered will often determine the rate of response. Long, take-home questionnaires, open-ended questions, and concerns about confidentiality (requiring signatures or asking personal questions) will result in poor response rates. In order to improve response rates, the following is recommended:

➢ Keep questionnaires short (no more than one page)
➢ Use simple questions
➢ Have questionnaires completed prior to, during, or immediately following service/activity

The following methods have been effectively employed in churches conducting a program:

➢ Printing the survey on the back of the church program
➢ Placing an insert in the church program
➢ Telephoning members who are absent from church service
➢ Presenting an announcement by the pastor, coordinator, or team member that encourages completion of the survey during or immediately following the service

It is imperative that the members be assured that all personal information offered will be held in the strictest confidence by the team, and the names of the individuals will not be included in program reports or presentations.

STEP NINE: ASSESSMENT AND SURVEYS

Survey forms should be distributed and collected by a team member, or the congregation can place them in a designated box. The data analysis from the survey results can give the program team insight for planning and can also aid in the evaluation process. The results of the survey data should be reported back to the congregation as soon as possible. A program insert summarizing survey results might be combined with an explanatory oral presentation from the pulpit.

Continuous assessment is critical. Here are some key tools:

Participant registration forms serve to gather demographic data on program participants. Other information that may prove useful are the participant's church name and affiliation, category (e.g., youth, parent, minister, member), and reason for participating in program.

Pre- and post-surveys measure and assess the changes in the level of knowledge and attitudes of all church and community participants. These surveys are used when implementing education classes that occur over a period of time in order to determine whether program participation has increased knowledge levels.

Monthly program reports determine the level of activity and provide details relative to quality, challenges, and recommendations for improvement.

Feedback forms report the feelings and opinions of participants.

Meetings held on a regular basis secure feedback from lay persons.

Training session attendance rosters aid in determining the number of active program participants and the retention rates of the participants.

Trainer's journal provides a descriptive log of the process of the program's development over a period of time. The process of program development is very important because it provides others with information about how a program progresses from the conceptual to the developmental and implementation stages. The program coordinator should collect data and information from reports and evaluations of both the program and the manual and summarize it in a journal for the committee.

The African American church, as the powerful and stable institution in the African American community, will continue to wield tremendous influence on the lives and lifestyles of men, fathers, and their families. The process of brainstorming, collaborating, developing, evaluating, and expanding church-based programs can be a rewardingly rich and formidable adventure for both the churches and the men, boys, and fathers being served.

PROGRAM CASE STUDIES

Our churches always seem to "reinvent the wheel" when it comes to ministry programs and initiatives. This does not have to be. There are many, many church-based efforts around the country that are blessed with incredible results and are able to point to the healing and restoration of individuals, families, and communities.

The next three chapters present program case studies. In this series of case studies, we are looking at three examples of programs that are working to fulfill the mission of the church: to evangelize and make disciples. We have tried to showcase a cross-section of ministry initiatives and to focus on some of the most critical issues for African American males today.

The first study focuses on prisons. The second will cover a comprehensive curriculum to address the needs of African American males (men, boys, and fathers) in the church. The third will cover an innovative program to reach adolescents via an intensive, long-term, small group process. These three case studies are excellent examples of how churches can interface with the boys, men, and fathers in their congregations. Hopefully, these detailed examples will spark ideas in your own ministries and congregations.

CHAPTER 5

CASE STUDY: REACHING MEN AND FATHERS THROUGH PRISON MINISTRY

You will notice that this section is the most comprehensive of the three case studies. There is a reason for that. A disproportionate percentage of African American men and fathers are incarcerated. The Bureau of Justice statistics reveal some alarming numbers:

- There are 34 sentenced African American male inmates per 1,000 African American men in the United States, versus only 4 sentenced White male inmates per 1,000 White men.
- Over the course of a lifetime, 28% of African American men will enter a state or federal prison.

A big part of the problem is recidivism—the frustrating phenomenon of prisoners who are freed to live in society but go back to their old ways, and once again end up in prison.

We believe that many African American men and fathers who are serving time in the nation's correctional institutions want to become productive participants in society upon release. However, well over half of them fail to make a successful transition back into society after release.

Research has identified several factors that enhance the chances of ex-prisoners to remain crime-free once released from prison.

Religion, which in many studies on recidivism has been a neglected variable, has proven to be an important factor in effecting change in the lives of those who want to leave a criminal lifestyle. Researchers and social scientists have theorized that religion affords a level of social integration and accountability that helps prevent antisocial behavior. That is where this case study comes in. The Transition of Prisoners®, or TOP program, focuses on integrating ex-prisoners into society by ensuring that they are immersed in caring relationships and communities.

TOP is a community-based program for prisoners and ex-prisoners at risk of returning to prison. The program encourages, trains, and supports local churches in building their capacity to effectively minister to prisoners, ex-prisoners, and their families. This is accomplished by facilitating a relationship between churches, ex-prisoners, the Department of Corrections, and other community organizations in order to reduce the societal, resource, and personal barriers ex-prisoners often face when attempting to make a successful transition back into society. The program also seeks to increase the ex-prisoners' level of attachment to social institutions in the community, thereby reducing their likelihood of resorting to antisocial behavior.

Let's take a comprehensive look at this successful program—one that can make a tremendous impact on our communities.

TRANSITION OF PRISONERS® (TOP) CASE STUDY

Program Summary

TOP is a church-based, Christ-centered prison aftercare program (Ephesians 1:22–23; 4:11–12) currently in operation in Detroit, Michigan. The program is founded on the belief that the only lasting change in a person's life comes from having a personal and vibrant relationship with Jesus Christ (2 Corinthians 5:17). In order to invoke this change, an individual needs to recognize that his past antisocial behaviors (sins) were in direct opposition to God's principles as contained in His Word (the Bible). The program views repentance from sin as an indispensable part of the process of transformation from a life of crime to a productive, crime-free life (Luke 13:3). Repentance, reconciliation, and renewal are strongly encouraged by the TOP staff and the church mentors who participate in the program. Through modeling by staff members, interaction with Christian mentors, participation in church services, and other program-sponsored events, program participants learn Christian values and behaviors. TOP intentionally recruits Christian inmates who share this philosophy to participate.

The Detroit TOP program has been providing aftercare services to ex-prisoners since 1993. Its primary objective is the rehabilitation of ex-prisoners through a comprehensive program of clinical intervention, church integration, referrals, and systematic mentoring.

During its seven years of operation, Detroit TOP has been able to achieve much. Through innovative church partnership, mentoring, and training activities, TOP has significantly reduced the risk levels and service needs of the participants during their first six months in the program. Currently, the recidivism rate is a low 10% for TOP program participants. The "graduation" rate for TOP participants is 35%—a significant number given its high-risk population.

Church integration is a central part of the rehabilitation process. Getting ex-prisoners into churches is pivotal to the social integration model and is also the strategy through which ex-prisoners are matched with church-attending mentors. Our discussions with the TOP staff and ex-prisoners indicate that for ex-prisoners who stayed beyond the probationary period, church attendance was almost 100%.

Mentoring training and mentoring link the TOP program to the community and churches and are the primary vehicles for diffusing the overall ministry of ex-prisoner aftercare. Clearly, the TOP program has made great strides in this area and has a network of churches that support the central idea of prison ministry and mentoring as essential aspects of discipleship. The development of professional tools for mentoring (Principles for Effective Mentoring of Ex-offender and New Mentor Basic Training) by the TOP staff and extensive national training of mentors are among the major accomplishments of the TOP program.

Referrals and partnerships enhance the program's ability to address job and drug treatment needs of ex-prisoners as well as addressing objectives of restorative justice. Evidence provided by the TOP staff indicates that they initiated or facilitated a number of partnerships apart from the primary relationships with area churches. TOP and its staff partner with a number of agencies to provide comprehensive services to its program participants.

Koinonia—Biblical Social Integration

The closest biblical equivalent to the concept of social integration is the concept of *koinonia*. *Koinonia* is an ancient Greek word that is used in several New Testament passages. It is most frequently translated as "fellowship." Fellowship with other Christians is not optional, but essential, to successful Christian living. One cannot be out of fellowship with other believers and experience fellowship with God. In the mind and teaching of Jesus, a church is a vital, living, dynamic fellowship of believers.

Christians in prison have the opportunity to experience a level of fellowship that few free-world believers will ever experience. Christians make up a relatively small, but very close-knit, segment of the prison population. There is a high level of accountability for the Christian prisoner. After all, in prison there is very little privacy. In the free world a person can secretly engage in an activity for long periods of time, but this is not so in prison. In prison, your habits and activities are known to practically everyone.

Also, the Christian prisoner faces a great deal of scrutiny from other inmates. When one declares himself to be a Christian, others begin to watch closely to see if there is validity in the claim. There is little tolerance for hypocrites within the prison population.

Christianity in prison is not as popular as many other groups and religious affiliations. Other inmates may look upon Christian groups with disdain. This creates a level of solidarity that is not known in the American church community. Christian prisoners depend upon each other a great deal for support and nurture.

These factors create an environment that promotes fellowship and spiritual growth. Christian prisoners spend a great deal of time in prayer, worship, and encouragement of one another. This environment allows them to experience a relatively high level of spiritual growth in prison. The average Christian prisoner may know more Scripture and spend more time in prayer and fellowship than the average "free" Christian!

However, once released, Christian ex-prisoners find themselves in a totally different environment. The high levels of accountability, solidarity, and support are gone. Without a proactive plan in place before release, few ex-prisoners will solidly connect with a church after release, and without this spiritual and social support, there is little else to do except to return to old friends, habits, and eventual failure.

In Acts 4, Peter and John were arrested and later released by the Sanhedrin. After they were released from jail, Peter and John went directly to their own company (believers). We as believers gain spiritual power from *koinonia* with other believers. Without it there can be no true spiritual power in our lives. Once released, ex-prisoners who fail to join with a group of believers forfeit the very spiritual power they need to remain drug and crime free.

The most important service that ministries such as TOP can provide to transitioning prisoners is connecting them with nurturing, receptive churches in the community. These churches become their source of spiritual and social support. When ex-prisoners come under the authority of a pastor, they have spiritual accountability. Within a holistic ministry context, the ex-prisoner can find not only spiritual solace, but also practical support in terms of locating housing, employment, and other essential services. This connection gives them the opportunity to not only love God, but to demonstrate love toward their brethren as well; thus living out the greatest commandment (Luke 10:27).

Through aftercare prison programs like TOP, the Christian ex-prisoner gains the spiritual power required to overcome the difficult obstacles to a successful transition back into the community. A nurturing, receptive church helps ensure that he or she will experience *koinonia*.

Spiritual Problems Require Spiritual Solutions

TOP staff acknowledges criminal behavior as a symptom of a sinful condition originating in an individual's *heart* (Matthew 15:18–19), due to their *old nature* (Romans 6:5–9), resulting from a direct violation of *the divine law of sowing and reaping* (Galatians 6:7–10). Addiction manifests itself within an individual's *soul* in the form of a *stronghold* (2 Corinthians 10:3–5). Following conversion where God crucifies the old nature, the *"works of the flesh"* (Galatians 5:19–21) remain within the soul and must be addressed through *mortification* by the Holy Spirit (Romans 8:13).

Understanding the root cause of criminal behavior (sin) and God's plan (sanctification) for change in the life of every believer, the TOP staff acknowledges the Word of God as being vital for that change (James 1:21). The Word of God is the Holy Spirit's primary tool for change in every believer's life and is key to deliverance and restoration from addiction (Ephesians 6:17). The anointed Word of God is the only existing vehicle that has the power to penetrate an individual's soul and spirit and judge the thought and intents of the heart where the root causes of addiction lie (Hebrews 4:11–12). Transforming the mind of the ex-prisoner is a must in both the deliverance and restoration process. Therefore, TOP has specialized group sessions designed to assist the ex-prisoner in developing a biblical perspective of addiction, deliverance, and the restoration process. Within those groups, a series of practical exercises have been specifically designed to assist the ex-prisoner in understanding, accepting, and appropriating God's plan for healing through His Word. God's Word is the primary instrument used with a substance abuse orientation, making it central to the core issues of addiction in the life of the ex-prisoner.

TOP PROGRAM GOALS

To build the capacity of local churches to assist ex-prisoners—We know that local churches already have prison ministries in place, but many of these efforts focus on providing outreach within the prison walls. TOP represents an opportunity to help individuals become productive once they leave the prison environment.

To raise the level of family cohesion for ex-prisoners—Family cohesion is another important way to prevent prison recidivism. Ex-prisoners who have strong bonds to their families tend to be more successful in finding and keeping a job as well as avoiding behaviors that might cause them to return to prison (Sampson and Laub, 1990). Helping ex-prisoners to enhance their family life helps these men successfully integrate back into society.

In cases where immediate family members are themselves dysfunctional, surrogate families may have to be established for the ex-prisoner. These individuals can include the mentor's family, other church members, or even positive friends that the ex-prisoner had already established.

To facilitate church integration for ex-prisoners—Affiliation with a strong church that pursues a holistic ministry concept can serve as a strong deterrent to recidivism. This is the kind of church that will provide or link the ex-prisoner to needed social services such as employment, counseling, or housing.

To facilitate job stability for ex-prisoners—Another key component of social integration is meaningful employment. Dale (1976) found that failure to find employment makes it four times more likely for ex-prisoners to return to prison. Sampson and Laub (1990) discovered evidence that episodes of unemployment lead to higher crime rates. Not only does work provide the income needed to sustain oneself and possibly one's family, but it also provides a sense of self-worth to individuals. Employment also occupies time that might otherwise be filled with detrimental thoughts and activities. These factors make helping ex-prisoners find meaningful employment an important component of this program.

To facilitate freedom from addiction through biblical means—As high as 98% of the TOP participants have been in bondage to substance abuse and trafficking. However, many ex-prisoners have a misconception of the nature of addiction and do not understand God's plan of deliverance and restoration (1 Corinthians 10:3–5). They view addiction as a problem of the past (prior to their salvation experience) and are unaware that the old desires and appetites of the flesh (Ephesians 2:3) will return for most once they reenter the community. Therefore, in conjunction with the mandatory Biblical Transformation and Restorative Group Process (appendix A) that addresses the root cause of addiction (sin), all TOP participants with prior histories of addiction (using and/or selling) are required to attend a specially designed **relapse prevention group.**

To identify housing opportunities for ex-prisoners—Securing adequate housing is often a need of ex-prisoners and their families. For those with families, this is especially true. Most prisoners are from low economic backgrounds. Many times when the head of household is incarcerated for an extended time, the family is forced into a lower economic situation. Under such circumstances, the ex-prisoner can return home to find their family living in substandard housing. Moving back into substandard housing located in an extremely high-crime neighborhood is a factor that may limit an ex-prisoner's chance for a successful transition. TOP seeks out those agencies or programs in the city that provide housing alternatives for low-income families. TOP staff researches these programs and agencies to identify programs that are suitable to meet the needs of the participants in the shortest length of time, least expensive manner, and with the best environments possible.

To equip ex-prisoners with new problem-solving skills—TOP has found that many of the men they have worked with have spent significant time in some kind of penal institution as adolescents and/or adults. These men have had to adopt values and survival skills that would allow them to live through the prison experience. This *prison culture* from which they have recently emerged is in stark contrast to the rules and norms of free society. Therefore, TOP has developed and implemented a group approach called the Biblical Transformation and Restorative Group Process. This process teaches the program participants how to address and solve problems in a way that is productive and consistent with the way free society behaves.

To promote and implement restorative justice principles—We have seen the power of restorative justice in action. It helps heal an entire community, not just the offender and the victim. It provides a needed opportunity for the offender to take responsibility and experience the spiritual freedom that results when **restoration,** not **punishment,** is the operative concept.

RESTORATIVE JUSTICE

Restorative justice is a concept with biblical roots:

"If a man steals an ox or a sheep and slaughters it or sells it, he must pay back five head of cattle for the ox and four sheep for the sheep" (Exodus 22:1).

Two ideas are fundamental in restorative justice: it (1) is harm-focused; and (2) promotes the engagement of an entire community.

Restorative justice views crime first of all as harm done to people and communities. Our legal system, with its focus on rules and laws, often loses sight of this reality; consequently, it makes victims at best a secondary concern of justice. A harm focus, however, implies a central concern for victims' needs and roles. Restorative justice begins with a concern for victims and how to meet their needs, and seeks to repair the harm as much as possible.

Restorative justice emphasizes offender accountability and responsibility—in concrete, not abstract, terms. Too often, we have thought of accountability as punishment—pain administered to offenders for the pain they have caused. Unfortunately, this is often irrelevant or even counterproductive to real accountability. Little in the justice process encourages offenders to understand the consequences of their actions or to empathize with victims. On the contrary, the adversarial game requires offenders to look out for themselves. Offenders are discouraged from acknowledging their responsibility and are given little opportunity to act on this responsibility in concrete ways. The "neutralizing strategies"—the stereotypes and rationalizations that offenders use to distance themselves from the people they hurt—are never challenged. So the sense of alienation from society experienced by many offenders, the legal process, and the prison experience only heightens the feeling that they themselves are victims.

If crime is essentially about harm, accountability helps the offender to understand that harm, to begin to comprehend the consequences of one's behavior. Moreover, it means taking responsibility to make things right as far as possible, both concretely and symbolically. As our fore-parents knew well, wrong creates obligations; taking responsibility for those obligations is the beginning of genuine accountability.

Restorative justice helps promote engagement by giving the primary parties affected by crime—victims, offenders, and members of the community—significant roles in the justice process. They need to be given information about each other and to be involved in deciding what justice requires in this situation. In some cases, this may mean actual dialogue between the parties, as happens in victim/offender mediation or family group conferences, to come to a consensus about what should be done. In others, it may involve indirect exchange or the use of representatives. In any eventuality, the principle of engagement implies involvement of an enlarged circle of parties as compared to the traditional justice process.

To put restorative justice in its simplest form: Crime violates people and the violations create obligations. Justice should involve victims, offenders, and community members in a search to identify needs and obligations, so as to promote healing among the parties involved.

PROGRAM STRATEGY
Identifying the Primary Client—Who Do We Serve?

TOP works by making the local church its primary client. The prisoners, ex-prisoners, and their families are in fact secondary clients. In order for the program to achieve this mission, TOP must effectively engage local churches in the community that desire to participate in this type of ministry.

The primary focus for Detroit's Transition of Prisoners® program has been African American churches because the population of Detroit is so heavily African American. Also African American males and fathers are the population that is most *at-risk* of returning to prison once released. Most churches in the African American community do engage in some kind of ministry to prisoners, ex-prisoners, and/or their families either by design or default. There is hardly a church that does not have at least one family with a family member who is in prison. Perhaps there is even a church member who is in prison. The participating congregations encourage those whom they minister to in the jails and prisons to visit their church upon release. Occasionally, ex-prisoners who have had no previous connection to a church may approach the church for assistance simply because the church is located in the community to which they have returned.

These churches will usually make some attempt to assist the prisoners, ex-prisoners, and their families who turn to them for help. Many pastors report that their attempts to help ex-prisoners have met with limited success. Some have met with utter failure and frustration as a result of having no previous experience working specifically with ex-prisoners.

Even those who have extensive backgrounds in working with prisoners within the institution find the job of working with ex-prisoners in the community far more challenging. Obviously, the perceived need and the willingness of churches to work with ex-prisoners is present. What are so often lacking, though, are the skills and resources to undertake this very challenging task.

TOP recruits churches that see the need to work with ex-prisoners in a more effective manner and are willing to enter into a partnership with the program. Once recruited, the church is asked to select one or more mentors from within their congregation. The mentors are then provided with approximately 10 hours of training in working with a person making a transition from prison to the community. Two-hour training sessions are provided on a bimonthly basis. Mentor support groups are also provided on a bimonthly basis. Churches and mentors are provided with an ongoing flow of relevant information, support with crisis intervention, and other relevant support services and training in order to build their capacity to assist not only their assigned TOP program participants, but other ex-prisoners who will ultimately seek them out for assistance as well.

Making the effort to build the capacity of the churches frees the TOP staff up to (1) work with a larger number of participants at one time; (2) give closer attention to participants who require a higher level of support; and (3) spend more valuable time performing important tasks which only they can perform.

CHURCH RECRUITMENT—STRATEGIES

African American churches are relational in nature. A great deal of importance is often placed upon establishing and nurturing relationships before any kind of partnership can be established. What matters most is not whether what is being offered to them is perceived as a viable tool that can be used to solve a problem, but that a trusting, respectful relationship is established.

Therefore "cold calling" (the practice of calling on a list of companies or organizations without a prior relationship being established or introduction being made) churches is usually **not** an effective way to recruit churches in the African American community *during the start-up phase of the program*. Recruiting churches in the African American community is a long process and often one that is very frustrating to those who do not understand the dynamics of the community. One must first of all begin this process with an honest respect and appreciation for this institution and culture. Often organizations with a condescending attitude toward the African American church have attempted to work with African American churches and have met with resistance and consequent failure.

Community-based programs that seek African American church involvement must work strategically to spur their participation. Here are the most important components of an effective strategy:

1) **Hire a church coordinator.** This person will take the lead in establishing and nurturing the relationship with the churches. He/she will also take the lead in the mentor training. This person must have strong interpersonal skills, as well as experience in church and cross-cultural relations.

2) **Begin with existing relationships.** To effectively recruit churches in the African American community, start with the churches you are familiar with who know you and work from there. Contact first by letter; then by phone call; and then make a personal visit to a pastor or church leader to begin building a case for the local church to work with the program.

3) **Utilize church associations and alliances** which are composed of pastors of the various affiliated churches. These groups are excellent sources of contact for potential TOP churches. Seek out the appropriate officials of these groups and request to be added to their meeting agenda to present the TOP program.

4) **Ask a participating pastor to identify other pastors** whom they feel have similar interests and would also be likely to commit their church to participate in the program. The pastor or church leader is asked to invite those identified to an event (e.g., breakfast, lunch, etc.) at which the program will be explained in detail and an appeal made for the pastors to make a commitment to at least attempt to involve their church in the TOP program at that time. A strong emphasis should be placed upon

how their involvement with the program will benefit their respective church. Some pastors may require a personal call in order to be persuaded to sign on to the program. Some church governments require that a board-level decision be made before such a program can begin at their church. Then, a formal presentation at those churches is required.

5) **Seek the insight and counsel of churches with existing experience** working with prisoners, ex-prisoners, and their families. This enhances the program and helps prevent unforeseeable problems. Focus groups, surveys, and personal interviews can all be used to accomplish this.

6) **Assure the churches of the competency of the program staff; give them as much information about their respective program participant as possible** (keeping in mind confidentiality issues). They must know that careful attention has been given to reduce risk factors that may result from bringing ex-prisoners into a church setting. Churches in the city are used to taking some risk in opening their doors and/or providing services to needy populations. They do not expect any endeavor to be totally risk-free. They must be supplied with a general profile of the participants involved in the program. We recommend that no more than one ex-offender be placed in a particular church unless there is good reason to believe that more than one will not overburden the congregation.

7) **Ask pastors to identify mentor candidates.** Most likely, the pastor will know which individual in the church he or she would like to fill this role. A profile describing the desirable characteristics of mentors may be useful in this decision. Their decision will ultimately be respected, unless there is concern over their choice.

8) **Formally recognize churches involved in the program** through public presentation of a certificate, dinner, etc.

9) **Engage in ongoing communications** with the local church through the church coordinator, case manager, administrative assistant, and director.

10) **Ask each pastor to complete a church survey** to help TOP in its evaluation of its program.

Refer to appendix B for a comprehensive series of action steps to take in order to effectively recruit churches.

PARTICIPANT RECRUITMENT AND SELECTION

TOP participants are recruited either directly from prison through referrals from Department of Corrections staff, including chaplains and assistant deputy wardens at level one facilities. Many TOP participants are recruited from Community Residential Program (CRP) managers, Tether (a program that allows enforcement officials to monitor a parolee's comings and goings from a remote site), and parole agents. Additional referrals come from volunteers, other Christian programs, TOP churches, or current/former TOP participants. Prospective TOP participants can apply when released into the community by the Department of Corrections, or when they are released with CRP, Tether, or parole supervision. The program is promoted via brochures and flyers in the prisons. Eligible participants are directed to contact their prison chaplain for a brochure, which includes a mail response card. Those who return response cards receive a letter instructing them to contact TOP immediately upon their transfer to the CRP or release back to the community.

In addition to the printed materials, TOP staff members also present the program personally to CRP residents. Interested parties complete an application and a series of assessments. Those materials are forwarded to the TOP CEO and case manager for final decision-making. Applicants found ineligible are sent written notification to that effect, along with a list of other possible service agencies.

ELIGIBILITY REQUIREMENTS— FIRST-TIME AND REPEAT OFFENDERS

- Participant must have been in a controlled environment for the previous 30 days (prison, CRP, substance abuse treatment, etc.).
- Applicant must have the agent send a copy of his parole eligibility report and presentencing investigation report to the program.
- Participants removed from TOP for committing a violent crime, threatening behavior, or a criminal sexual offense are not eligible for readmittance to the program.
- Participants returned to prison for technical rule violations (TRV), stipulated to detox/substance abuse treatment retain participant status.

- Participants returned to prison who did not complete their initial orientation period or were dismissed from the program for lack of participation may be readmitted after TOP staff review of their (1) prior participation; (2) new crime committed; (3) relationship with TOP assigned church; (4) recommendations from PF and DOC staff; and (5) personal interview with TOP staff.

Anyone readmitted to the program must complete a new 30-day orientation period.

PROGRAM STAFFING AND STRUCTURES

To achieve ongoing success in a local church-based aftercare ministry, it is critical to maintain an effective church relations component and a workable infrastructure to ensure that ongoing program needs are met. Effective strategies and processes for partnering with local churches must be in place. It is crucial that the program build those partnerships to a relatively high level of mutual respect, trust, and commitment to the mission of the ministry (Isaiah 42:6–7; Matthew 25:36).

Case Manager

The Case Manager facilitates the case reviews during the staffing. Each staff member has the opportunity to make suggestions about future transitional issues and referrals and to raise questions about past and present transitional goals and objectives. The Case Manager also assists in identifying and addressing critical areas of transition and in establishing crisis interventions. He or she reviews the initial application and provides telephone support to the assigned mentors.

Church Relations Coordinator (CRC)

The sheer volume of contacts involved in effective church relations, including the need for continuity, accountability, and availability all combine to demand a full-time staff position for every 30 or so churches. Although volunteers may have the skills, gifts, motivation, and commitment to perform as CRCs, rarely would they have the availability. This work requires 40 to 50 hours per week. It requires working days and often evenings, weekends, and Sundays.

In world missions work, the church has learned that the most effective ministry takes place when indigenous leadership is developed and supported. We believe that aftercare ministries working with non-White churches could greatly benefit from this lesson by hiring indigenous people, who have been called of God to the work, to fill the position of CRC. These people are equipped with a lifetime's accumulation of knowledge regarding the cultural and social values, practices, and sensitivities of the congregations in question.

RESOURCE CHURCHES

Resource churches are those churches that are outside of the city of Detroit geographically, but have a heart for ministry in the city. These churches do not serve as primary TOP mentor churches because of their geographic locations. However, they have a willingness to share their resources with those "front line" ministries providing spiritual nurturing and positive social support systems for ex-prisoners.

Many urban churches that are committed to the spiritual and social support needs of the program participants are unable to meet their material transitional needs (e.g., housing, employment opportunities, clothing, etc.). By providing for some of these transitional, material needs, resource churches enhance the effectiveness of aftercare programs.

Here are some of the roles that resource churches can fill:

1) **TOP Contributor.** These churches contribute financially on a regular basis to TOP.
2) **TOP Partner.** These churches make a commitment of people and resources to:
   a) Sponsor periodic events designed to recruit other resource churches.
   b) Sponsor regular events which bring resource churches and TOP churches together to fellowship and exhort one another to continue their ministry to ex-prisoners.

c) Provide emergency assistance to program participants who have no mentor, or whose church is unable to provide the needed resources.

d) Participate in a standing committee to plan, organize, and co-ordinate the efforts of the various resource churches (i.e., create a job bank, secure housing sources, provide ongoing re-cruitment, etc.).

This partnering between resource churches and TOP mentor churches not only enhances the effectiveness of aftercare programs in ur-ban areas, but also facilitates the building of relationships and reconcili-ation between city and suburban churches.

CHURCH ADVISORY COUNCIL (CAC)

TOP has established a council of churches consisting of pastors and other church leaders committed to the program. Every church that par-ticipates with TOP is eligible and is encouraged to designate a pastor or church leader to participate on the council. The Church Advisory Coun-cil (CAC) is to represent and reflect the various Christian denominations that are present in the Detroit area. The members of the CAC act as li-aisons between TOP and their church associations. They serve as an advisory group for the CEO of TOP regarding church-related issues. The CAC is to hold the CEO accountable for church-related issues and prob-lems that may rise during the administering of the program. This en-sures that TOP remains focused on and sensitive to the needs and concerns of the churches involved with the program.

The CAC gives guidance in regard to fundraising within the church. The members of the CAC help to identify other churches that may be interested in working with the TOP program.

The council chairperson or a designee serves as a full member on the TOP Board of Directors. That person is responsible for representing the needs and concerns of the CAC.

CHURCH REIMBURSEMENT—
GOOD SAMARITAN FUND

TOP feels that it is important not to place a financial burden on churches that may already be under financial strain. Therefore, we have established a church reimbursement fund called the Good Samaritan Fund. This makes participation with TOP less prohibitive for churches with few financial resources.

Based on Luke 10:35—"The next day he took out two silver coins and gave them to the innkeeper. 'Look after him,' he said, 'and when I return, I will reimburse you for any extra expense you may have.'"

Purpose—The purpose of the Good Samaritan Fund is to demonstrate the love of God to those who have fallen along life's roadside (ex-prisoners) in a tangible fashion. This fund will reimburse the churches up to $500.00 per program participant for any approved expenses they may incur as they help the ex-prisoner(s) assigned to their church. These expenses can include items such as transportation, personal hygiene, or leisure/recreational activities that the mentor and the TOP ex-prisoner may pursue; or other categories approved in advance by the church. *Program participants will not be eligible for the Good Samaritan Fund until they have completed their 30-day orientation period with the TOP program.*

MAINTAINING THE BOND—
AN EFFECTIVE STRATEGY

The stress and strain of spiritual warfare that accompanies ministry, particularly prison aftercare, is challenging; therefore, many people tend to get burned out or drop out before long. Unlike in-prison ministry, aftercare requires personal interaction with the ex-offender in the community without the security measures that a prison affords. The ex-offender attends the mentor's church and the mentor must spend recreational time with the ex-offender outside of church activities. It also requires that mentors be available at times that are inconvenient and unscheduled. There are as many reasons why people leave the prison aftercare ministry as there are for other areas of ministry. The main point is that people will leave, thereby necessitating the recruitment and training of new volunteers. This fact often means the forming of new partnerships with new churches also.

The average church in America has less than one hundred adult members in regular attendance, and our experience indicates that the number of men is often less than 30% of the total. Therefore, there is an enormous demand made on the time of available men in the church (95% of the ex-offenders are men and will require male mentors). This fact often has much to do with the need to constantly seek new mentor candidates and also new churches. Often a church will only have one or two men who are qualified *and* available *and* have a heart for this ministry. When these men cease to be active in this ministry, for whatever reason, the church is unable to replace them immediately. Therefore, an ongoing partnering effort is needed to sustain the ministry.

Once a church commits to a partnership, the building of the relationship between that church and the ministry becomes of paramount importance. The fact that the urban churches are relational in nature requires a serious commitment of time and human resources on an ongoing basis, to establish and nurture those relationships to a relatively high level of trust, respect, and commitment. It also requires personal contact with the pastor, church leadership, and/or the mentor(s) on a regular basis. *More* is certainly better in this regard.

The high level of personal interaction needed to develop and maintain trust, respect, and commitment requires that the CRC be a full-time paid staff person. It has been our experience that to effectively maintain 25–30 churches with approximately the same number of mentors, the CRC needs to invest approximately 800 hours per year in activities involving personal contact with the pastor, mentors, and/or other members of the church. These activities should include visiting church services, attending church events, program-related problem resolution meetings, providing ongoing training, frequent phone contacts with mentors, regular mentor meetings/events, etc.

Here are some practical administrative activities to engage in to continue to cement and solidify the relationship with partner churches:

a) Create and maintain a contact log for all church maintenance contacts.

b) Where requested, make TOP presentations to potential mentors in an effort to assist the pastor in identifying mentor candidates.

c) Contact mentor by phone within 30 days after mentor match to check on how the relationship is developing and to see if initial issues are being addressed.

d) Design and facilitate regular mentor meetings (for training updates, exhortation, and fellowship) on a bimonthly or quarterly basis.

e) Visit all partner churches at least twice a year for a Sunday service and/or church event.

f) Assist the Director in recruiting a Church Advisory Council (CAC) from among the pastors of partner churches.

g) Coordinate quarterly CAC meetings.

h) Assist in planning and conducting annual ministry events (i.e., picnics, CAC-sponsored fund-raiser/recruitment events, Christmas parties, etc.).

i) Assist mentors and pastors in planning and conducting graduation ceremonies for program participants.

j) Mediate conflict between participants and mentors.

MENTORING

The mentoring component is essential for ex-prisoners to make a successful transition back into society because of the need of ex-prisoners to have a friend who models prosocial behavior. This is needed in light of the fact that ex-prisoners have spent a significant amount of time in the presence of friends and associates who model antisocial behavior.

Churches with strong backgrounds in prison ministry generally provide a team of mentors who are assigned to work with each participant. Other churches may have only one assigned mentor. Each mentor receives extensive training in the issues surrounding working with prisoners, ex-prisoners, and their families. Mentors begin working with participants and possibly the families of participants while the participant is still in a community residential program. The mentor becomes a bridge between the church in the institution and the church in the community.

Mentors are asked to make a commitment to work with a participant for a period of six months at a time. However, these matches may well result in lifelong relationships. Of course, the intensity of the mentor support needed by the participant should diminish with the passing of time.

One important aspect of mentoring is that the mentors model pro-social behavior. In addition they should be accessible to the participant to reinforce the principles he is exposed to in church, Bible study, fellowship groups, etc. Mentors are a point of accountability for the participant. Also, they are able to assist the participant in making decisions when they are faced with stressful situations

We asked a former prisoner and sociologist to give us the benefit of his unique experience on this issue. He wrote the following:

The prison environment and the prisoners' unofficial code of conduct in many instances have become an integral part of the ex-prisoner's self-concept. When a person enters a prison he is stripped of his pre-prison identity. He is forced to identify himself as a prisoner and to accept or incorporate the prisoner value system, at least while he is incarcerated. That is to say that people who are incarcerated are around people who reinforce anti-social behavior which tends to have a lingering effect. The ex-prisoner can possibly hold those negative values after he is released into the community.

This may affect the ex-prisoner's attempt to transition back into society. Placing ex-prisoners around people who model pro-social behavior negates the deviant value system ex-prisoners incorporate while in the prison environment. Thus, the mentor and other positive significant others reinforce the pro-social behavior of the ex-prisoner. Mentors should serve as role models and perhaps more importantly friends to the ex-prisoners.

Participation in TOP will benefit the mentors as well as the participants. The mentor also has a need for friendship as well as the desire to help another individual. This type of bonding could prove to be an enriching experience for the mentor. It is the basis of a lifelong friendship.

Although some churches will have one mentor assigned to work with each program participant, it is most desirable, we've found, that there be a team of two or more trained mentors working with the participant. This team approach to mentoring has several benefits: It provides for trained backup in the event the "primary" mentor is unable or unavailable to assist the participant; it provides additional sources of counsel with whom the participant has established a rapport; it multiplies the number of prosocial role models with whom the participant personally interacts; and it tends to accelerate the participant's social integration into the life of the congregation.

The mentor receives extensive training in the issues surrounding working with prisoners, ex-prisoners, and their families. The mentor is matched with the program participant after he completes his 30-day orientation period, and will serve as a "bridge" for the participant from the institution to the church.

Mentor Training

Mentoring is a very important factor in the success of the TOP program. Mentors are the primary contact persons for the program participant and his family regarding issues of problem resolution. Special attention is given to the selection and training of mentors.

Pastors/churches are supplied with a general profile of mentors. However, the church is ultimately responsible for the selection of the mentors.

Ten hours of training are required for certification as a TOP mentor. Mentors initially receive three hours of training. Part I, a three-hour training, consists of five modules:

- TOP Overview
- Mentor Responsibilities
- Department of Corrections—Supervision Levels
- TOP Mentor Match Protocol
- Transitional Planning—from Prison to Society

Part II, a seven-hour training, consists of three modules:

• Developing a Biblical Perspective of Relationships
• Knowing the Enemy (spiritual warfare)
• Relationship Building (dynamic of mentoring)

In addition, two-hour bimonthly mentor edification meetings are held to provide mentors with both support and additional skills training.

TOP has devised specific mentoring materials for its purposes and makes use of additional supplemental material, as well as speakers on various issues such as the African American family for ongoing training.

Mentor Match Process

The mentor match process is critical to TOP's success. As with program participant-church matches, careful attention is given to mentor-program participant matches. Program participants and mentors are matched on as many areas as possible including theological persuasion, temperament, etc. Here again we find an advantage in the team approach to mentoring. The involvement of more than one mentor increases the likelihood that the participant will bond with a trained mentor; even if the bond is with a "secondary" mentor, the foundation for effective mentoring is established.

Once the Church Relations Coordinator is notified of a participant's acceptance, he or she moves to schedule a meeting with the mentor and church pastor. At this meeting, the CRC reviews the participant's transition goals, discusses immediate needs, reviews the mentor's job description, and discusses roles and accountability. The mentor signs a covenant form that commits them to the program. The importance of confidentiality in all matters related to the participant is emphasized.

Mentor Support and Edification

Mentors often suffer from a lack of attention from the program—they feel too much "on their own" and lose perspective on their work as mentors. They may feel they are failing, but don't want to admit it.

Experience has shown in some programs that regular support meetings—which may include some training, but whose real purpose is for the mentors to relax and encourage each other—keep mentors vitalized in their mission with the program.

Mentor support is provided via: the bimonthly training sessions, where mentors can share challenges and frustrations; the TOP Church Relations Coordinator and Case Manager, who provide one-on-one support and counsel; and a referral list that allows the mentor to direct their assigned TOP participant for resources and services. Mentors are formally recognized through presentation of certificates in a public venue or at a special TOP event.

CHAPTER 6

CASE STUDY: ROSEDALE PARK BAPTIST CHURCH SCHOOL OF MINISTRY

INTRODUCTION

Rosedale Park Baptist Church in Detroit, Michigan has developed an innovative way to reach men and fathers. Their "School of Ministry" is a two-year curriculum that teaches Scripture and its application, builds relationships within and between families, and takes adult men and fathers through a comprehensive series of topics that address spiritual, social, and economic development.

The church inducts a new group of members every six months (nine per group), and holds classes for all participating groups in the same location at the same time. This way, members who have already begun the classes can interact with new class members and share the wisdom they have learned. We have found that this approach yields additional benefits. The men and fathers who participate have developed friendships outside the framework of the classroom. This builds relationships and results in members feeling a sense of mutual accountability, facilitates informal prayer groups, and allows members to discuss personal issues and challenges openly and honestly. We fully intend for this initiative to give birth to our next generation of leaders.

Rosedale Park operates under the philosophy that we need intergenerational programs to build effective leaders. The men and fathers who participate in classes and other programs are of varying ages; this enhances communication between the generations and allows for a smoother transition of leadership from one generation to the other.

Here is a look at the curriculum:

Background

The women at Rosedale Park Baptist Church (RPBC) have developed an effective program of small group discipleship clusters. A similar effort is needed for the young and older men and fathers.

Purpose

The purpose of the RPBC School of Ministry is to enhance the effectiveness of both established and emerging church leaders by:

1. preparing members to communicate their personal faith, and
2. equipping members to function as role models at home, at church, and in the community.

Goals

1. To develop men who pray, study, and teach the Word of God at home, at church, and in the community.
2. To develop husbands who:

    • Listen attentively,
    • Speak with authority,
    • Develop the family's purpose,
    • Establish goals for the family, and
    • Spend time developing intimate relationships with their wives.

3. To develop fathers who listen, show affection, and spend time with their children.
4. To develop leaders who practice faith, wisdom, and love within their homes, at church, and in the community.

Educational Objectives

On completion, the graduate should be able to:

1. Apply biblical knowledge with faith and obedience in their home, church, and community.
2. Support and be sensitive to the pastor, church staff, and members.
3. Identify and develop spiritual gifts for leadership roles in the ministry of the church.
4. Communicate their personal relationship with Jesus Christ with people outside the church.
5. Teach and train Christians to mature in their faith and obedience to God.
6. Develop the biblical knowledge in communicating with different racial and ethnic people.
7. Recognize when problems arise and be able to refer to individuals, books, tapes, and other resources to assist in solving the problems.
8. Plan, manage, and evaluate educational and ministry projects in the church.

Educational Outcomes

On completion, graduates should demonstrate:

1. Qualifications to be an elder, pastor, or staff person in the church
2. A strong family life
3. Strong interpersonal skills and relationships
4. High morals and integrity
5. A willingness to serve others
6. The ability to teach the Word of God and defend the faith
7. A lifestyle that demonstrates maturity in the faith

8. A willingness to do ministry with a variety of racial and ethnic people

Schedule

- Two years for certificate/diploma
- Classes are divided into six two-day sessions per year: Fridays from 6–9 P.M. and Saturdays from 9 A.M.–3 P.M. (this allows the men to participate in other church activities without becoming overloaded with their duties as husbands, fathers, and employees)
- Practicum* the first and second year
- Each session covers two subjects for a total of nine hours

* See page 86 for detailed description of Practicum

Qualifications

- Rosedale Park Baptist Church member in good standing
- Must have a personal relationship with Christ
- Approval of the pastoral staff
- Commit to a 2-year training period
- A member of Rosedale for a least one year or have completed the new members classes

ROSEDALE PARK BAPTIST CHURCH
COURSE SEQUENCE

Duration: Two Years

COMPREHENSIVE COURSE LISTING

Title of Course	**Course Description**
Bible and Theology	The study of God.
Introduction to Strategic Planning	A process of thinking long range.
Introduction to Management and Leadership	Areas of training for the leader who is to serve.
Biblical Counseling	Various skills, techniques, and applications of Christian approaches.
Church Doctrine	The development of doctrine in the church.
Evangelism and Discipleship	Methods for sharing with people about Jesus Christ and growing in their faith and obedience.
Introduction to Urban Ministry	Methods of serving people in the city.
Old Testament Survey	The major beings, institutions, and themes of the Old Testament.

Title of Course	Course Description
New Testament Survey	The centrality of Christ and His teachings.
Life Cycles of the Church	Different stages in the life of a church.
RPBC Practicum	Using the cell group or the small group method to evangelize and disciple our families.
Teacher Training Techniques	Examine techniques which create a successful learning environment.
Public Speaking	The current applications of speaking skills.
Marriage and the Family	Successful family and basic social institutions with cultural variations.
How to Lead Small Groups	Different methods for leading small groups.
Cross-Cultural Communication	Examine a variety of cultures to allow students to gain perspective.
Authority and Servanthood	The importance of authority and servanthood in the church.
Pastoral Epistles	Different leadership roles in the church.

Title of Course	Course Description
Personal Financial Management	Acquaint students with principles and concepts of basic financial planning.
Practical Christian Living	Truth of the Scriptures pertaining to Christian life in the family, church, and community.
Missions	Biblical view of global missions and practical applications.
Personal Communication	Examine the process of communication and interpersonal relationships focusing on the role of the self.
Computer Usage	History and purpose of computers and the Internet.
Principles of Networking	Learn how people serve people.
Spiritual Gifts	Discover one's spiritual gift for serving in the church.

ROSEDALE PARK BAPTIST CHURCH
SCHOOL OF MINISTRY—PRACTICUM

Vision Statement: To become models of strong biblical families led by men and fathers by the year 2003.

Mission Statement: To teach, train, and mentor in order to foster open communication, mutual support, and accountability that strengthen our families.

Method: Family Conference Table

Modules:

Prayer
Daily prayer with spouse/children
Corporate prayer with group
Individual

Counseling
Weekly topic

Devotions
Individual (Daily)

Communication (Personal and Family)
Respond God's Way
Family Conference Table (Weekly)
(see description on next page)
Husband/Wife Communication

Discipleship
Study of Discipleship
Older Teaching Younger
    Siblings
Children

Evangelism
Jesus' Teaching
Family Outreach
Backyard Bible Study

Personal Testimony

Bible Study
Old and New Testament
What Does the Bible Say?
Detail Ability of Finding
    Biblical Solutions
Show How It Can Be Done

Mutual Respect	Relationships
Relationships Between Fathers and Sons	Sensitivity
Discipleship Process	Understanding the Subtleties of Relationships—How to Pay Attention

Textbooks:

Title	*Author*
Staying Pure	Stephanie Perry Moore
Sober Faith	Stephanie Perry Moore
The Black Family: Past, Present & Future	Lee June, Ph.D.
Men to Men	Lee June, Ph.D. and Matthew Parker
Women to Women	Norvella Carter and Matthew Parker
Evangelism & Discipleship in African American Churches	Lee June, Ph.D. and Matthew Parker
Sheep in Wolves Clothing	Joseph Williams
One-Year Bible Study	Navigator Press
Operation Timothy	Christian Businessmen's Committee

Other Books:

Understanding Cultural Diversity	*Maximize Manhood*
Growing Kids God's Way	*Man in the Mirror*
Walk Through the Bible	

Time Period: Two Years

Family Conference Table:

One weekly meeting that lasts a minimum of 15 minutes and a maximum of 60 minutes. Within this time frame men should:

1. Have talk time with the family.
2. Discuss needs of the family members.
3. Have a time of prayer.

CHAPTER 7

CASE STUDY: EXECUTIVE CLUB "THINK TANK" TO IMPACT ACROSS THE GENERATIONS

INTRODUCTION

In 1949 when I was still a child, my mother died and left my father with two children to raise alone. Dad provided for our spiritual development until 1971, when he also passed away. I found myself turning to three special individuals: Barbara Walton, Lloyd Blue, and Tom Skinner. I asked them to be my spiritual parents and mentors. Fortunately for me, they agreed. I have been blessed.

These three people have taught me much, and I always said that one day I would pay my debt to them by taking on a group of young people to provide the same kind of guidance and support I was so generously given.

The Executive Club, started as "The Generals" in 1993, included 25 young people in grades 8 and 9. A group of us in ministry approached a number of churches and asked if we could take on a group of young people to mentor and nurture spiritually.

We met on Saturdays from 9 A.M.–2 P.M. and brought professionals and leaders to speak about many topics. We included a time for Bible study, and frequently took the young people on field trips to area universities. We engaged them in service projects and in initiatives where they could discover and hone their skills and talents.

Of that first group of 25, 20 finished the program and 18 went to college. We still work and have contact with 12 of those young adults today.

In 2001, we changed the name of our group from "The Generals" to "The Executive Club"—a nod to changing times and changing ideas of what would be respected and revered. We now have eleven 13–15-year-olds going through a similar curriculum, and have secured funding from a local bank through the federal Community Reinvestment Act, which mandates banks to provide funding for community-based initiatives. We are looking for these young people to accomplish as much as their predecessors did.

Here is a brief look at the Executive Club's mission statement and curriculum (for more detailed information, feel free to contact the Institute for Black Family Development at 313-493-9962).

Executive Club Mission Statement

To provide a Christ-centered program designed for young emerging leaders to assume major responsibility in their own or our nation's primary institutions and organizations.

Objectives

- The students will learn how to make informed decisions regarding college enrollment and how to achieve success in college.
- The students will learn responsibility towards themselves, their family, and society through instruction in self-esteem, family structures, strategic life planning, civics, peer group dynamics, financial planning, and communications.
- The students will develop a working knowledge of the fundamentals of employment training (e.g., resume writing, job finding skills, interviewing, and employer-employee relations).
- The students will know how to write a logical, organized, and credible career plan.

- The students will be exposed to a comprehensive mentoring program designed to enhance their leadership skills for the business world.
- A minimum of 50% of students will enroll in a college or university.

PROGRAM DESCRIPTION

Tract I

The Life Skills Curriculum is designed to promote a responsible and independent lifestyle as the student matures into adulthood. The modules include:

Self-Esteem—This class will increase awareness regarding self worth, and social, mental, physical, and spiritual development. Effective strategies will be shared for developing a healthy self-image to replace any negative images.

Family Structures—This class will help students understand the family and its various roles. It will also help students develop coping and relating skills.

Strategic Life Plan—This class will encourage development of a practical, meaningful plan and will incorporate education, career, family life, and personal development.

Civic Responsibility—This class will provide practical legal and political information.

Peer Dynamics—This class will teach peer counseling techniques to address crisis areas such as suicide, violence, pregnancy, AIDS, peer pressure, substance abuse, and sexual abuse.

Personal Finance—This class will guide students through the complicated world of personal finance. Students will learn how to open a bank account, how to handle credit, and how to approach large purchases such as homes or cars.

Independent Living—This class will help students explore the world after high school graduation. It will teach "what it takes" to survive away from home.

The Social YOU—This class will explore the relational side of life, including how to make and keep friends, and whether, who, and when to marry.

Communications—This class will promote positive interactive skills in the areas of multicultural communications, conflict, and stress management. The development of these interactive skills will help students handle conflict and become more sensitive to others.

Tract II

The Employment Training Curriculum is designed to teach preparatory employment information and encourage proper employment skills. The modules include:

Personal Assessment Inventory—This class will inventory the student's life, helping them discover what they are qualified to do presently; what they have the aptitude to do; and what they may enjoy doing in a job setting.

How to Find a Job—This class will explore the various methods of job hunting. Instructors will discuss approaching employment agencies and self-promotion/marketing.

Filling Out Forms—This class will teach students how to fill out various forms such as job applications, 1040 EZ tax forms, W-2 forms, and other job-related documents. An inability to complete forms can hinder employability.

Longevity in the Marketplace—This class will discuss how to keep and advance in a job. Topics will include timeliness, attitude, appearance, and "going the extra mile."

The Job Interview—This class will prepare students for the interview process.

Professional Etiquette—This class will explain the dos and don'ts in corporate American, including how to dress, how to work with a supervisor, and how to fit into the business/corporate climate.

The Résumé and Cover Letter—This class will instruct in the development of résumés and cover letters for maximum impact in the job search process.

How to Get the Career You REALLY Want—This class will allow students to evaluate the content of what they have learned, including their personal assessment inventory; and direct their writing of a plan outlining their strategy for entering the career of their choice.

Tract III

The College Preparation Curriculum is designed to provide information to help students make meaningful and informed decisions regarding college enrollment, and how to achieve success in college. These module include:

Motivation to Study + Successful School Habits = Success—This class will encourage students to be committed to study and will share helpful study skills.

Preparing for the PSAT—This class will teach effective test-taking techniques related to the PSAT, and administer to students a simulated PSAT.

Reading for Comprehension and Speed—This class will teach speed-reading with a special emphasis on comprehension. The students will perform drills to increase both reading speed and comprehension.

Term Papers and Tests—This class will explore the various methods of writing a term paper and will highlight the differences between the styles. It will also teach effective test-taking strategies.

Preparing for the ACT—This class will teach how to effectively prepare for and take the ACT, and administer a simulated ACT test to students.

Financial Aid—This class will outline the various forms of financial aid available to the new college student. A particular emphasis will be placed on filling out the federal financial aid form.

Self-Discipline and Other Failure Factors—This class will take a good hard look at why students drop out of college, including academic reasons. Students will be given positive patterns to follow for success in college.

How to Choose a College—This class will examine three areas: financial, academic, and moral/spiritual issues to consider when choosing a college. Students will perform a college search based on these three considerations.

Tract IV

The Entrepreneurship Curriculum is designed to help students acquire a basic working knowledge of how to succeed in business by developing and writing a logical, organized, credible business plan. Modules include:

What Is an Entrepreneur?—This class will introduce students to the world of small business and self-employment. Students will take a test to see if they possess the qualities necessary to become a successful entrepreneur.

Best Business Brainstorm—This class will involve the students in a search for the type of business they would like to start and help them evaluate the feasibility and marketability of their idea.

Career Day—This class will allow several successful entrepreneurs to share with students their personal pilgrimage and journey, providing meaningful and usable success strategies.

Marketing Your Business—This class will help students strategize effective marketing techniques. Students will learn how to "sell" themselves by identifying their specific skills and determining their competitive edge.

Researching Your Business—This class will take students on a tour of the Detroit Public Library. The tour will focus on the business section and introduce the materials and resources available for effective business/market research. Students will then have an opportunity to research specific information for their business idea.

Developing the Business Plan—This class will cover the following material to develop a complete business plan: the narrative (executive summary, business description, industry analysis, target market, promotion management, personnel, competition); the financial data (cash flow projections for three years, balance sheet, break-even analysis, capital equipment list, accounts payable and receivable list); and supporting documents (personal information including résumé, tax returns, credit report, references, maps).

Obtaining Capital—This class will expose students to the financial aspects of granting business loans from the bank's perspective. Students will learn how to compile a thorough, well thought-out business loan application.

CHAPTER 8

RESOURCES

These books and articles will help guide your ministry efforts to African American males. They have been selected for their variety of perspectives, detailed research, and useful information.

BOOKS

Andelin, Aubrey. *Man of Steel and Velvet.* Publisher: Pacific Press, Santa Barbara, Calif.

> A book that teaches men to be men. Helps young, single men to visualize their future role, and mature, married men to examine their effectiveness as husbands and fathers.

Bennett, Lerone. *Before the Mayflower.* Publisher: Penguin USA., East Rutherford, N.J.

> A history of the presence of Blacks in the United States before the beginning of enslavement/indentured servitude in 1619.

Branch, Taylor. *Parting the Waters: America in the King Years, 1954–63*.
    Publisher: Simon & Schuster Inc., New York.
    Pulitzer Prize-winning book, a sweeping historical account of the
    Civil Rights Movement. Covers the role of the church as both a sup-
    portive institution and as an impediment to civil rights progress.

Dickens, Jacqueline and Floyd. *The Black Manager.* Publisher: American
    Management Association, New York.
    Prescriptive study on Blacks in management positions. Gives pro-
    fessional development advice to Black managers, and describes the
    challenges they face in a predominately White environment.

Freeman, Joel and Griffen. *Return to Glory.* Publisher: Renaissance
    Productions, Woodbury, N.J.
    Highlights significant accomplishments of African descendants and
    exposes the racist cover-up of those accomplishments. Analyzes suc-
    cess factors in African American achievement, and promotes cross-
    cultural understanding.

Kunjufu, Jawanza. *Countering the Conspiracy to Destroy Black Boys,*
    vols. 1–4. Publisher: African American Images, Chicago,.
    Describes Black male development and its challenges both within
    and outside the family, with an extensive discussion on school, com-
    munity, and society. Suggests strategies that families, churches, and or-
    ganizations can employ to ensure the development of spiritually
    grounded, emotionally healthy, and well-educated young men.

Kunjufu, Jawanza. *Adam! Where Are You: Why Most Black Men Don't
    Go to Church.* Publisher: African American Images, Chicago.
    Chronicles current and historical reasons for the dearth of African
    American men in the church. Includes a chapter on the relative suc-
    cess of Islam in attracting African American men.

Lane, Eddie B. *Reclaiming the Village: The African American Christian Man.*
Publisher: Black Family Press, Dallas.
Discusses practical strategies for helping develop whole, Spirit-controlled African American men. Covers issues of socialization, manhood, family, authority, and conflict resolution.

June, Lee. *The Black Family: Past, Present and Future.* Publisher:
Zondervan Publishing House, Grand Rapids.
Historical perspective on the Black family, with prescriptions for future policy and practice.

June, Lee and Matthew Parker. *Men to Men.* Publisher: Zondervan
Publishing House, Grand Rapids.
Advice from 16 Black professional men on critical men's issues, including marriage and family, reconciliation, community restoration, and the criminal justice system.

Richardson, Willie. *Reclaiming the Urban Family.* Publisher: Zondervan
Publishing House, Grand Rapids.
Practical help for evangelism and outreach in the urban community from the pastor of the successful, Christian Stronghold Baptist Church in Philadelphia, Pennsylvania.

MAGAZINE/NEWSPAPER ARTICLES

Earl, L. and N. Lohmann. (1978). "Absent Fathers and Black Male
Children" [Notes for Practice], *Social Work,* 23, pp. 413–415.
Discusses the impact of fathers who do not live inside the home on Black male children.

Mendez Jr., G. A. (2000). "Incarcerated African American Men and Their
Children: A Case Study," *Annals of the American Academy of
Political & Social Science,* 569, 86.
Report of a study conducted by the National Trust for Development of African American Men to try to determine the attitudes of incarcerated men toward fatherhood while they are incarcerated.

Discusses the finding that incarcerated men are willing to participate in programs to improve relationships with their children and families.

O'Donnell, John M. "Involvement of African American Fathers in Kinship Foster Care Services," *Social Work,* September 1999, vol. 44, issue 5, p. 248ff.
Describes the extent to which 74 African American fathers participated in services on behalf of children placed in kinship foster homes (homes of the children's family members) because of abuse, neglect, or dependency. Explores possible explanations for the low participation and identifies practices and policies to increase the father's involvement.

Rodney, E.H.; R. Mupier. (1999). "Behavioral Differences Between African American Male Adolescents with Biological Fathers and Those Without Biological Fathers in the Home," *Journal of Black Studies,* 30, 45.
Depicts behavioral attitudes of African American adolescents raised by single-parent families in the United States. Identifies causes of behavioral disturbance in adolescents, and investigates the importance of the father's role in child rearing.

Roy, Kevin. "Low-Income Single Fathers in an African American Community and the Requirements of Welfare Reform," *Journal of Family Issues,* July 99, vol. 20, issue 4, p. 432ff.
Presents information on a study that examined the influence of welfare reform in the paternal involvement of low-income single African American fathers.

Tobesman, R. (1997). "Fatherhood and the Black Man," *New York Amsterdam News,* 6/14/97, vol. 88, issue 24, p. 6.
Black-owned and operated newspaper looks at fatherhood as it relates to African American men. Includes information on the role of social service agencies, and suggestions for African American men to support their children. Features comments from Dr. Louis Sullivan, former United States Secretary of Health and Human Services.

Toth, Jr., J. F.; X. Xu. (1999). "Ethnic and Cultural Diversity in Father's Involvement," *Youth and Society,* 31, 76.

Uses national data to examine American father's participation in child rearing for children aged 5 to 18 years, according to race, ethnicity, and gender/family ideology. Results show that fathers' involvement is a function of the specific combinations of race, ethnicity, and cultural ideologies.

Veneziano, R. A. "Perceived Paternal and Maternal Acceptance and Rural African American and European American Youths' Psychological Adjustment," *Journal of Marriage and the Family,* 62, 123.

Explores the differences in self-perception between rural African American and European youth, and its relationship to parental acceptance by either father or mother. Examines whether father or mother have a greater impact on psychological adjustment as reported by youth.

Zimmerman, M. A., D. A. Salem, and K. I. Maton. (1995). "Family Structure and Psychosocial Correlates Among African American Adolescent Males," *Child Development,* 66, 1598–1613.

Examines the effects of family structure (parental presence by gender, extended family in home) on African American adolescent young men.

CURRICULUM INFORMATION AND AVAILABILITY

For further information about the Executive Club, contact Matthew Parker at 313-538-1180 or 313-493-9962.

For more detailed information on the curriculum and methodology of the Rosedale Park Baptist Church School of Ministry, contact Matthew Parker at Rosedale Park Baptist Church at 313-538-1180.

CHAPTER 9

WHAT WE MUST DO: A MANIFESTO FOR CHANGE

WHAT WE MUST TEACH OUR BOYS

We must teach our boys to appreciate their African heritage. We must display before them our heroes, to let them know that many people have paved the way for our blessing and success.

We must tell our boys how to speak to people, look people in the eye, hold their heads high, and believe in their hearts that they are somebody. People who are confident make changes. People who are confident are the most likely to succeed.

We must remind our boys that they are loved and lovable. And we must start by teaching our boys that, too. A loved child can face anything. A loved child is better able to accept God's love, because he has experienced the beauty of the parent-child relationship.

We must teach our boys that real men don't just produce children—they *father* them.

WHAT WE MUST TEACH OUR MEN

We must demonstrate to our men by example that cheating, stealing, and abuse of their wives or children is not God's way.

We must teach our fathers that they will never help their sons become men unless they first become men. We must stress to them that their own failure to take responsibility will be the biggest barrier to their son's emotional, spiritual, psychological, and sociological development.

We must teach our men what a real man is:

- a **priest**—one who leads the spiritual development of a family,
- a **provider**—one who is able to provide for of a household's basic needs,
- a **protector**—one who knows how to keep bad influences, people, and circumstances away, and
- a **lover** (for husbands only)—one who loves his wife as his own flesh, and remains faithful to her in mind and spirit as well as in the body.

We must teach our men that the failures of their own fathers does not mean that they are destined to fail their sons. We must not use our own dismal past as an excuse. At some point, we have to break these generational curses—why can't it be you?

We must teach our men that real men respect and cherish all women as special.

We must teach our men that real men call their wives if they're running late, and have no problem telling them why. They come home at a decent hour because they respect their wives and children. We must reverse this macho psychology that "she doesn't need to know—I'll get there when I get there."

We must teach our men that real men never, never lift a hand to *any* woman.

We must teach that real men do not just talk to their parents (the obligatory once a week phone call); they take care of their aging parents and make sure they live lives of quality until God calls them home.

We must teach our men that real men guard their tongues. James

3:6–8 says that the tongue, while a "little member," has the power to bless and to curse and can set on course the fires of hell if unbridled. That gives us reason to be sober about what we say.

We must teach our men that real men move from lust to love, from "shacking" to building a relationship that he can present before the very face of God without shame or embarrassment.

We must teach our men that real men seek to own rather than rent, to save rather than spend, to give rather than take. We must work toward the elimination of debt. The borrower serves the lender; an overload of debt can even hinder your ability to serve God, your family, and your community.

WHAT WE MUST TELL OUR BOYS, OUR MEN, AND OUR FATHERS

We must tell our boys, our men, and our fathers how special they are every day. They won't get that anywhere if they don't get it at home.

TOP® BIBLICAL TRANSFORMATION AND RESTORATIVE GROUP PROCESS

The Biblical Transformation and Restorative Group Process rests on the premise that every individual is born spiritually dead and alienated from God. Establishing and maintaining a personal relationship with the Father through accepting Jesus Christ as Lord is the key component within this process. The transformation and restorative group process is threefold in purpose. It is designed to equip the ex-prisoner for an effective Christian lifestyle of worship, service, and character development.

The first phase of the group process is focused on creating awareness in the ex-prisoners' life for a need for change (repentance; 2 Corinthians 7:9–10) through sharing the gospel message. Next they are provided with an opportunity to act on the need for change through acknowledging Jesus as Lord (faith; Romans 10:9–10). Once the ex-prisoners have established a relationship with God, the process sifts to providing them with: (1) an understanding of the spiritual transformation (regeneration; 2 Corinthians 5:17) which has occurred; and (2) acceptance of their right relational standing with God and new identity in Christ (justification; Titus 3:5–6).

The second phase of the group process is based on restoration and is designed to equip the ex-prisoner with a biblical belief system by renewing their mind (Romans 12:2). The biblical belief system will enable them to mature in their new position, making an outward change in behavior and conduct that corresponds with the inner change made by God (sanctification). The ex-prisoner learns not to conform to the patterns of the world through character development. The group process allows the ex-prisoner to address difficult transitional issues from a biblical perspective. The ex-prisoner is also introduced to the basic spiritual disciplines: the Scriptures (meditation, study, and memorization), prayer, praise/worship, fellowship, and fasting during this phase of the group process.

The third phase of the group process is designed to introduce the ex-prisoner to the fundamental attitudes necessary for spiritual growth: submission, humility, trust, self-control, vigilant defense (1 Peter 5:5–8), and educate the ex-prisoner in the spiritual warfare involved in the Christian lifestyle. The group process facilitates a lifestyle of spiritual and emotional development. During this phase they are taught the value of "sowing to please the Spirit" (Galatians 6:8) and not "walking in the flesh" (mortification; Romans 8:13).

The fourth and final phase of the group process is designed to assist the ex-prisoner in understanding God's purpose for their Christian life through service to the Lord. Preparing the ex-prisoner for service is accomplished through introducing them: (1) to the Great Commission (Matthew 28:19–20), and (2) to the spiritual gifts, which gives them an opportunity to identify their gift and understand God's purpose for their lives (Romans 12:6–8).

The group process is comprised of a combination of didactical teaching, group interaction, testimonies, and individual exercises designed for practical application of each biblical principle. The group process is open-ended and progressive, allowing each new group member opportunity to enter a session at their individual level of development.

TOP® CHURCH RECRUITMENT AND RELATIONS ACTION STEPS

STEP ONE

1. Prepare list of prospective pastors/churches.
2. Create introduction letter developed for pastors.
3. Create program summary paper developed for pastors.
4. Mail letters and program summary paper to pastors.
5. Make follow-up phone calls to pastors to set up face-to-face meetings.
6. Make personal presentations to pastors to explain the program and how their church can become involved.
7. Make church presentations when requested by the pastor and the church.

STEP TWO

1. Set up focus group meeting with pastors, church leaders, and other community stakeholders. The purpose of this meeting is to allow the pastors, church leaders, and other stakeholders to give input

into the program as well as for the TOP staff to answer any questions and address any concerns they may have regarding the program.

2. Send follow-up letters to pastors thanking them for attending the meeting and support given to the project.
3. Develop mentor profile.
4. Send letter informing the church of first mentoring training workshop.
5. Send mentor profile sheet with letter to give pastors a guideline for selecting the volunteer mentor.
6. Develop Good Samaritan Fund (Church/Mentor Reimbursement Fund).
7. Conduct mentor training.
8. Send questionnaire to churches to evaluate their attitude toward ministering to ex-prisoners and their families in the local church.
9. Send mailing to churches articulating benefits the churches may derive from being involved with TOP.

STEP THREE

1. Mentor matches begin between volunteer mentors and ex-prisoners.
2. Identify suburban churches to serve as resource churches.
3. Develop a Church Advisory Council including pastors from each church providing mentors and/or resources for TOP participants.
4. Ask churches committed to TOP to designate a Sunday in the month as TOP Sunday. Provide information about how they can pray for TOP and ways they can support the mentor and ex-offender.

A letter and certificate will be given to each church commending them on their involvement with TOP. This will be presented in the morning service by a TOP staff person or council member in that local church or given to the pastor of the church.

a) Compose an introduction letter which:
- gives a brief overview of what you do (as their partner)
- gives a biblical rational for why and how you do it
- requests an appointment with the pastor to present more information

b) Compile a mailing list of pastors/churches from available publications, such as church directories, yellow pages, etc.

c) Perform mass mailings of introduction letters prepared and sent out to targeted pastors/churches

d) Create a database for mailing list and a contact log to record all subsequent contacts

e) Record all contacts with appropriate remarks from initial contact through the formal commitment made by the pastor/church

f) Make follow-up phone calls requesting meetings with pastors

g) Record all appointments on partnering calendar of CRC

h) CRC attends all appointments with package including
- PF statement of faith
- Detroit TOP key components sheet
- a brief written history of Detroit TOP
- mentor job description
- summary of Good Samaritan Fund
- TOP brochure (brief program overview)
- mentor covenant
- mentor church commitment
- Prison Fellowship ministries brochure
- Detroit TOP newsletter

i) CRC requests commitment and signing of commitment statement at conclusion of presentation

j) If a commitment is made, offer help in mentor candidate selection process (willing to make presentations to potential candidates) and schedule follow-up contact

k) If no commitment is made, schedule follow-up call (time frame varies)

l) Enter all contacts throughout the partnering process on the contact log

Other Great Titles from Lift Every Voice

Planting Seeds of Hope

How To Reach A New Generation of African Americans with the Gospel

African American youth are looking for role models they can trust. The network of support is already in place. God has placed many of His most compassionate workers among today's African American young people. This book is written to help youth workers, pastors, parents and others who care about reaching young people with the hope of the Gospel.

ISBN: 0-8024-4197-1

God Just Showed Up

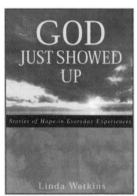

God Just Showed Up is a compilation of various short stories written by 19 talented writers and Christian educators on their personal experiences of how God changed their lives. Included is the life story of Curtis Martin who before being known as a running back for the New York Jets football team, and the NFL 1995 Rookie of the Year, lived in fear of not reaching his 21st Birthday because of the violence in his life, and how God changed his life.

ISBN: 0-8024-6591-9

Taking Care of Business

Establishing A Financial Legacy for the African American Family

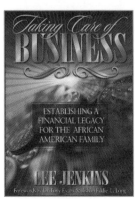

Most people wrongly believe that the money they earn belongs to them, and they have a right to do with it as whatever they please. However, the Biblical view of stewardship involves both ownership and accountability. Lee Jenkins guides us in setting goals in the areas of family, faith, friends, finance and fitness. In addition to providing guidance and direction, he reviews goals that make us think strategically.

ISBN: 0-8024-4016-9